The Entrepreneur's Code

The secrets, struggles, & eventual victories of visionary entrepreneurs

Charles Ajayi-Khiran

9. 2. 19

Printed in the United Kingdom.
First Printing, 2017

Hardcover ISBN: 978-1-904582-09-0
Softcover ISBN: 978-1-904582-10-6
eBook ISBN: 978-1-904582-11-3

Published by Charles Khiran International
Charles@charleskhiran.com
http://charleskhiran.com

Ordering Information:
Quantity sales. Special discounts are available on quantity purchases by corporations, associations, and others. For details, contact the publisher at the address above.

Dedication

This book is dedicated to my wife, Chyna; my son, Jordan; and daughter, Camille. Thank you for allowing me the space to create this work. You have my love and total devotion.

Acknowledgements

I would like to pay homage to some of the people who have influenced and contributed to, in one way or another, my entrepreneurial journey and success over the past 27 years. There are many people who directly or indirectly inspired my thirst for knowledge and my zest for the abundant life.

Some, I read about their work and their incredible achievements while I cheered from a distance as I dreamt of uncommon possibilities. Many of them, I had the privilege of knowing personally and working closely with. And many became my heroes, very good friends, and acquaintances whom I was able to study and shadow at close proximity over the months and years.

Firstly, I would like to give all glory and honour to the Great 'I AM', who gave me the gifts and talents to execute my divine call.

Here are some outstanding entrepreneurs and super entrepreneurs who have inspired me in one way or another over the decades. Some have been my inspiration over the years, some mentors, and some good friends. I would like to single out a few for special mention:

Reginald F. Lewis (RIP), Art Williams, Jeff Roberti, Jay Martin, Brigg Hart, Daryl Utterbach (RIP), Jim Rohn (RIP), Kerry Daigle, Dan Holzmann, Bob & Sue Burdick, Gary Chamberlain, Shay O'brien, Robert Kiyosaki, John Maxwell, Tony Elumelu, Bishop David Oyedepo, Matthew Ashimolowo, Damon Buffini, Earl Graves Snr, Mike Murdock, Bob Safford (RIP), Myles Munroe (RIP), Brian Tracey, Dr Patricia (Pat) Francis, Anita Roddick (RIP), George C. Fraser, Dr Bill Winston, Fred Stege, Steven K. Scott, Robert G. Allen, Bishop Wayne Malcolm, HRH Mahmood Ahmadu, Hakeem Bello-Osagie, Oprah, Earvin 'Magic' Johnson, Kanya King, Wilfred Emmanuel Jones (The black Farmer), Elon Musk, Richard Branson, Les Brown, Earl Nightingale (RIP), Ursula Burns, Michael Jordan, Professor Pat Utomi, Strive Masiyiwa.

Note to the Reader

The subject of entrepreneurship is a very broad and popular one, attracting rarefied admiration from many quarters. Depending on your personal experience, you will probably think fondly or sadly about this subject matter.

Many people have fantasized about becoming an entrepreneur, and many still have titled themselves naively as one, without truly understanding the full implications.

There are many fine books on the subject of entrepreneurship, books that delve into the greater details in terms of the complete cycle of conceptualizing, planning, financing, and eventually launching out.

My focus, however, is more concentrated on the inward journey toward entrepreneurial success. I provide inspiration and empowerment to manage the challenges, losses, loneliness, confusion, repeated doubts, and despondency. I show you how to silence the doubts and bounce back from failures before achieving any measure of success.

This book goes into detail, including periods of regular

self-doubt when you wonder if your idea is ever going to fly or not, moments when you are the only one who believes you can make it against an avalanche of disbelieving well-wishers who encourage you to go get a proper job, moments of deep introspective analysis which lead you to quit several times and pack it all in, because you have not earned a decent income for a long time and the wolves are at the door with only so many months and years left at the end of your limited or non-existent funds.

So the purpose of this book is to give you, the entrepreneur or budding entrepreneur, hope and encouragement from somebody who understands the journey and who has been an entrepreneur for over 27 years with varying degrees of successes and failures.

This book will, hopefully, accompany you on your journey toward entrepreneurial success and to let you know you are not alone. It should provide you with strength, encouragement, and advice for the journey ahead towards high achievement.

With best wishes for your glorious future,

Charles Ajayi-Khiran

August 14th 2017,

London UK

Table of Contents

Chapter One:

My Journey To Entrepreneurship

> "Only the weak close shop, quit, and pack it all in when the going gets really tough"
>
> -*Charles Ajayi-Khiran*

> *The size of your success, is mea-
> sured by the strength of your desire, the
> size of your dream, and how you han-
> dle disappointments along the way*
> *- Robert Kiyosaki*

My entrepreneurial journey began in earnest in 1990 at age 26. My colleague, Mark Weston, and I made the decision to launch our photocopier and fax machines dealership in the city of London. This was our second venture, as the first one we started based in Woolwich, South East London, only lasted for just under a year before we packed it in and went back to full time jobs as salesmen.

At that point, we were both top salesmen for Canon, Nashua, and Toshiba photocopying and fax machines. We saw the huge sums of money that were possible with that line of business. More interestingly, we were generating a lot of business for the company we worked for as experienced salesmen. We were paid a basic salary with the bulk of our earnings coming from our hefty commissions.

So he and I reasoned we could be enjoying all that money by launching our own dealership, and as experienced sales men we could run the company and also be in the field producing personal business as well. The plan sounded good to us and, after several months of discussing and planning, we sold ourselves on the idea and decided to launch out.

We approached the owners of the company we worked for and persuaded them to take a chance on us. We asked them to handle all the servicing of the equipment, which was the real backbone of the business and generated true residual and real income. The servicing and back end catered for the supplying of toners, cartridges, replacement parts and engineer call outs and general maintenance.

They agreed with, and liked, the proposition. They felt with the size of business we were bringing in that it could be very lucrative for them, too. We were ecstatic, as the on-going servicing of the equipment was the most important and expensive part after the sale was secured. Having secured this very important part, we contacted the equipment manufacturers, Canon, Toshiba, and Nashua, the leading players in those days besides Xerox, and persuaded them to take a gamble on us and give us the opportunity to sell their equipment.

After some great negotiations, they liked our dynamism, energy and big aspirations, and they said yes. They also gave us favourable credit terms. They believed we could help increase their market share, branding, and positioning in a very competitive UK market.

After securing the deal with the manufacturers, we recruited massively and attracted 22 sales people, some experienced, and others we took on as trainees. We paid them a whopping 60% commission with no basic salary, and leased the sporty version of Ford Escorts (XR3) cars for them. For those of you who remember, the Ford XR3's were the boy racer cars in those days. We operated our business out of premises in Long Lane, near Smithfield's, in London. We felt like millionaires, even though we were just getting started.

The joy of just travelling daily to the rarefied environment of the city and our colour coordinated offices on the 5th floor with a beautiful view was oh so satisfying. Our hearts were full of dreams of taking a slice of the huge London market.

In our first 18 months of trading, we found out that everyone was getting paid besides us. We kept drawing money from the company and could not afford to pay ourselves salaries. Our debt began to mount up sharply, and we borrowed to put back into the company. Our credit cards, by this time, were completely maxed out.

This was not going according to plan. We began to realise very quickly that we chose the wrong time to enter the market, as the UK was experiencing one of the most devastating recessions in the early nineties.

I remember one poignant situation when we had succeeded in signing this very big deal in Covent Garden with a particular company. The company was huge. They occupied a very large, beautiful glass building, and they leased a couple of big machines from us. We had hired a van to transport the machines to their premises for demonstration purposes, hoping they would fall in love with the machines and keep them.

They loved the equipment and signed the deal. The deal was worth £230,000 over a 60 month lease and we had a profit of £60,000 built in. I remember going back to our offices that night and popping open a bottle of champagne, celebrating the deal and toasting to our greater future. This was early winter 1991.

Everything was depending on this deal, £60,000

was a huge sum of money in 1991. Plus, Christmas was 8 days away. However, we discovered that we could not get the deal accepted by any of our regular leasing companies like Schroeder's because, as beautiful as the client's building and interior looked, the company was actually insolvent. We became desperate and began farming out the deal to brokers; anything to get the deal accepted and to get paid some money.

Even with the exorbitant brokers rate, we were ready to accept anything they offered hoping we could still end up with a satisfactory profit. Shockingly we discovered that no one would accept it nearly one month later.

I remember sitting in a spirit of abject despondency one night in the office about 7.30pm. I had the worthless piece of paper in my hands, with huge sums written on it, but worthless. I looked out of the window and was almost tempted to jump. I had to snap myself out of that suicidal thought. It was really that bad. This was our last lifeline as we had maxed out everything.

We just could not afford to stay afloat anymore. We needed money to live. We earned far more money working as salesmen, and we were almost bankrupt operating as business owners. So, after Christmas, we sold the business for almost nothing to our former employers. They took it over and gave us jobs as joint General Sales Managers for one of their new acquisitions in Canary Wharf. I was relieved to be back in employment and earning regular income without having the responsibilities of shouldering the day-to-day decision making of business ownership.

BACK TO WORK AND BANKRUPT

However, we incurred huge debts. Plus, I also signed a promissory note with a repayment schedule, which I defaulted on terribly, and the creditors came after everything I owned. I also owed American Express, as I had borrowed on my charge card, which I attempted to use as credit card. In those days, Amex provided cheque books to accompany my charge card. I used some of the cheques to pay other creditors.

Anyhow, Amex had enough when I could not pay back the debt quickly enough and bankrupted me. I later found out that it was more beneficial for Amex to bankrupt me as they could claim back the debt from their insurance, as opposed to allowing me the luxury of paying back over an extended period of time.

I had never been in this position before and was spending a lot of time at courts fighting one debt or the other. I remember one of the most frightening and distressing moments of my life was when the insolvency chap invited me in and went through the process of what happens when somebody is made bankrupt.

He wanted to know about every single thing I owned, every penny, every account, property, car, investment and the rest. Fortunately, I did not own very much, but it was still a harrowing experience as I could not tell a lie about anything. I was eventually declared bankrupt in court to my amazement. At this time, I was in a daze as everything was moving too fast and I wasn't sure when I would be able to see some sunlight again.

Anyhow, I fought back and went back to court 5

weeks later and explained to the judge the circumstances. I was able to prove that Amex was being very unfair and that it was in their best interest to bankrupt me. I showed the judge payments I had already made, and my repayment proposal to clear the balance, which I had sent to Amex.

The judge this time around was an absolute angel. He took it upon himself to defend me as I had no lawyer. He basically did most of the work himself and threw out Amex's case. He tore up their additional claim for extra expenses incurred while working on my case.

The amounts were in the thousands of pounds. The judge told them it was very unfair, and how could they expect me to pay for all that? He finally reduced their expense claims from thousands of pounds to just under £500!

Honestly, it was a miracle. God was fighting my battles for me. The stress had simply been too much and I was on my last legs. Fortunately, the judge annulled the bankruptcy, and I was a free man again.

Anyhow, life settled a bit. I was now employed full-time as general sales manager and earning a regular income. I was getting used to a semblance of sanity and a little peace.

While I was working full-time, I also took on a part-time job as a bouncer or doorman in a night club down the road from my flat in west Kilburn. This part-time job paid good money, approximately £400 for 3 nights work weekly. I kept up this punishing regime with the great social life that accompanied this kind of life style and I was able to save money again.

Then one night, I went to rescue a young lady being harassed by some drunken guys in the dimly lit dance floor. Before I knew it, one of the guys had smashed a large glass of beer on my face. The glass shattered, narrowly missing my eye. I had a cut from my fore head down through my left eye lid. For those who have seen me in person, they will notice a scar on my forehead to this day.

I was rushed to the hospital in Park Royal North West London, and by this time, my face had swollen like a balloon. Anyway, I had it stitched and was discharged. That was the end of the doorman work for me, as I thought it wasn't worth losing an eye, for I had a more professional job and a brighter future to look forward to.

NATIONAL SAFETY ASSOCIATES

Then, in late 1992 August my closest friend, then Ola, introduced me to National Safety Associates (NSA), a multi-billion-dollar American network marketing company which manufactured water treatment systems. Ola was in financial services sales with Allied Dunbar and was doing quite well, and I was doing quite well as general sales manager for the office equipment company. I turned down the opportunity several times, as I did not fancy flogging water treatment machines, and could not grasp the concept of MLM at that time.

Ola kept sending me copies of his impressive monthly cheques. I could see they were growing on a month-by-month basis. I still was not tempted as I was doing quite well in my job and trying to heal from the bruising of my last entrepreneurial venture.

However, I required Ola's help with some complex paperwork to enable me get a mortgage for a piece of property I was purchasing. So being the closer that he was, he said no problem. There was only one condition. The condition being that I took a close look at NSA.

I said yes, and that was how I got involved in what proved to be one of the biggest learning experiences and most successful ventures in my life. I developed my NSA business on a part-time basis alongside my full-time job. I immersed myself in personal development with the help of my great up-line sponsorship leaders Donald Afun and others, who kept supplying great materials for our personal development.

I began aggressively growing my team, providing motivation and leadership, and I really threw myself into this business. I saw it as a way to realise my financial and time freedom dreams. I did this for 23 months and moved quickly up the ranks. Within that time, I succeeded in growing my income to £50,000 a year on a part-time basis with my NSA franchise. This matched my full-time income.

I also saw the potential to double my income if I gave it more time and attention. Then, on the 23rd month, I decided to make the leap to full time with NSA and never looked back. 10 months later, now working full-time, I had produced the required volume with my awesome team which had grown to thousands of people.

I was able to achieve the pinnacle of success in NSA- National Marketing Director (NMD). I had succeeded in building teams of many thousands of people in several countries across Europe. Seven months after qualifying as an NMD, I also succeeded in producing the required volume of $1.5 million dollars with my huge team. I was appointed a President's Advisory Council member (PAC 10).

I was now one of the world's elite and in the top 5% of the world's NMD's. My expense allowance alone provided by the company was up to £24,000 per year besides my income, which had now hit the 6 figures bracket.

I was now 29 years old, enjoying all the finer things of life, massively engaged in personal development, and was spending a small fortune in leadership and sales trainings to keep my mind finely tuned to all things success and leadership. I was reading several books a month on leadership, including biographies and auto-biographies of highly successful individuals. My customized Mercedes sports AMG car was a library in itself where I listened to over 10,000 hours of audio tapes on success mastery.

I drove long distances every month, working with my leadership team right across Europe. I got on the ferry from England to Calais, France and drove through Gent, Sint Niklaas in Belgium, right through Hertogenbosch, Amsterdam in Holland, continuing to Aachen, Dusseldorf, Munich, Frankfurt, etc. These were my more frequent routes.

Sometimes, I would take the ferry direct with my car to Hook van Holland and drive the short distance to Den Haag or the Hague and get to my destination that way. I was away approximately 10 days every month by car to these cities building my leadership teams. I was away quite a lot from my new wife whom I married in 1995, the same year I achieved the NMD position. Other times, I would travel by plane to other parts of Europe growing the team, supporting the emerging leaders, and producing the volume.

NSA was an average person's franchise, so it was a real entrepreneurial enterprise. It was my own business within the larger multi-billion-dollar company. At this time, I was also living the high life, driving beautiful cars, wearing tailored suits, and doing lots of international travel. I enjoyed this magical life for a while until trouble struck again.

NSA, unfortunately, received some bad press because of a new and innovative nutritional product they launched. This was the early days of Juice Plus, a powerful nutritional product made up of many fruits and vegetables in capsules. The media got wind of it and attacked it, denying its potency and efficacy.

THE BEGINNING OF ANOTHER END

As a matter of fact, we had two television attacks within two weeks of each other from the Food and Drinks programme and Watchdog. I was clearly unhappy with the way NSA responded to these terrible and untrue attacks. They did nothing. When some of us directors questioned them on the wisdom of taking such a soft approach, they said it was pointless to go on TV and defend with the truth.

The advice from their PR company was to just leave it and it would go away on its own. Due to these attacks, our UK business was rocked negatively. Many of us who were senior players experienced unimaginable losses. I lost over 1000 people from my organisation in the UK alone, and this started a chain re-action of many more leaving. I saw my income drop from 5 figures monthly to less than £800 per month.

I tried for over 26 months to rebuild, but it was just not happening. This was between the years 1998-2000, and within six months, I experienced a series of terrible events. My marriage, already in trouble, suffered irreparably and this led, eventually, to a divorce.

My business was gone, or at least, what was left of it. My health was massively affected. I was diagnosed with high blood pressure and diabetes suddenly, probably due to the immense stress.

Yet again, I lived on my savings for many months while trying to bounce back, but I soon realised I had to do something else. It just wasn't happening anymore. So after 11 plus years with NSA, I quit and tried sorting out all the chaos around me.

Incidentally, Juice Plus went on to become one of the most powerful nutritional products in the market, generating billions of dollars many years later as the science was proven.

BACK TO WORK, PART II

Now I had to go and look for something to do to bring in money. I did some casual short term work here and there, like selling electricity during the privatisation exercise in the UK, while looking for something I could sink my teeth into and finally succeeded in applying for an opening in the city for a role as a coach/senior consultant to middle and C-Level executives with the world's leading career management and coaching company, Bernard Haldane's, in 2001.

The advert wrote "If you are not afraid to earn £100k plus working as a consultant with senior executives, then apply." I promptly applied and was invited for an interview.

Two of us made the shortlist, me and another chap. The managing consultant called me into his office and told me they made a decision to go with the other guy, as he was already experienced in the industry and would require less training.

However, he said to me, he had never been challenged like I challenged him. He said he appreciated my senior level experience plus my entrepreneurial zeal, and he wanted me as well. He asked me to give him 3 days to persuade the CEO and the chairman based in New York to allow him to create another position for me, as they only had one opening. I told him no problem and that I would wait to hear from him.

Two days later, he called me excited and asked if I still wanted the position. He told me that it was mine if I was still interested. I started the following week. They had to create an office for me on the 5th floor as there wasn't room on the consulting floor downstairs.

This is what I teach people all the time. If you are good at what you do, opportunities will be created for you where they previously did not exist! I went for a lightening training course, learning the lingo of marketing and coaching senior players, and within 6 months made it to the consulting floor.

In my first year, I finished at number 5 in the country out of nearly 50 consultants across the UK. By years 2-3, I had the biggest office and became the most experienced in the London office, achieving the top 2-3 positions in the UK. I was in that role for nearly 6 years.

It was a self-employed role, running my own operations within the international company. I was able to interview over 3000 of some of the most successful executives from the UK and Europe who came to London looking for an opportunity in the very dynamic London jobs market. The trouble is, the more senior someone is, the more difficult to find a new role, and many of these senior people needed a lot of support.

They would come to us and pay us a lot of money to support their efforts in finding opportunities. The average time it took for a C-level executive to land a role in the early to mid-2000's was anywhere from 6 months to 18 months, depending on seniority. If a CEO came to us, then the average time was 8 – 24 months.

We provided very plush offices in the city and the West End of London with the latest technology for accessing the invisible jobs market along with a coach who would work with them to boost their confidence and provide expertise.

The more senior somebody was, the less chance they had of securing a role through the normal channels of recruiters, or newspaper adverts. Most senior roles are unlocked through understanding how to work the unadvertised roles and getting good at providing high visibility and networking.

They would come to us and we would coach them on how to present their CV's, from 5-8 pages down to approximately 2 pages of achievement-orientated marketing documents. We would also teach them how to interview for success. They were more acquainted with sitting on the other side of the desk and now, all of a sudden, they are the ones being interviewed.

Many of these senior players are used to running the show, usually in very high powered environments, but have lost their roles and don't know what to do with themselves. For the men, they have played all the golf, fixed the shed, or anything else that needs doing at home. The wives are not used to seeing them at home all the time.

These men will do anything to be back again at work, and for the women, it is no different. Women at these senior levels are driven and get bored outside of their dynamic work environment. I, however, saw more men than women. I would guess the ratio was about 80% men to 20% women.

LAUNCHING CHARLES KHIRAN INTERNATIONAL

As I was consulting, I set up my professional speaking and training business, 'Charles Khiran International,' on the side in 2003. I had been speaking for much longer at huge company events, sometimes to crowds of many thousands, and delivering trainings, too, for at least eight years prior. Now, however, I was going to be doing it professionally.

I began to seek opportunities part-time to market my speaking and training services. I was putting in an average of 10 – 12 hours a day at this point, between my consulting work and building my part time speaking business. I enrolled in the Professional Speakers Association in London, and joined Toastmasters International to polish my speaking skills.

When I showed up at Toastmasters and delivered my numbers 1 – 3 speeches, they asked me if I was a professional, as my delivery was at a very high level. I then quit Toastmasters shortly afterwards, as I picked up what I needed from that great organisation and did not complete the full program, as my speaking skills were already very strong. I also got my executive coaching certification first from Florida in the USA, and a couple of years later from the UK.

I began to volunteer my services to many organisations for free. My only interest was to get seen and heard. I networked with colleagues from Toastmasters and other organisations and learned how to create visibility. I remember one of the key individuals that really helped me at the start was Kris Akabusi, the former Olympian and successful motivational speaker. I went to visit him in his office in 2003 and asked him how I could go about marketing my services, and he gave me some good advice.

Little by little, my speaking business began to grow, but it was hard work, as I did it the old fashion way. I wasn't a TV celebrity, nor a sports star, and neither was I a bestselling author. Any of these would have given me strong exposure and a soft landing. In the absence of these, I had to do it the hard way, one gig at a time.

Then in 2005, I was introduced to Citi-Solutions, a UK subsidiary of the American giant insurance and investment company, Primerica. My pastor and close friend, Rev Carlton Williams, stopped by my office in Regent Street and asked me to accompany him to a meeting taking place on Oxford Street, which was just round the corner.

I said okay and we both went down together to the meeting. When we got there, we were received by Jeffrey Lestz and were seated. The legendary American, Bob Safford (RIP), was presenting.

The moment he set eyes on us, he directed most of his presentation to Carlton and I. At the end of the presentation, we were introduced to Bob by Jeff Letsz, who was the most senior player in the UK for Citi-Solutions.

CITI-SOLUTIONS

Bob wanted to meet with us privately. The next day, Jeff created time in Bob's diary for 30 minutes, which ended up becoming a 2-hour meeting. Now, Bob was a giant in the industry. At that time, he was 73 years old. He was a mentor to John Maxwell, the leadership guru, and so many other big players. Bob averaged $2-3 million dollars a year and had amassed over $100 million dollars in his career with Primerica through direct earnings and investments.

You could not say no to Bob. Carlton and I were hooked. He demonstrated to us how we could both be million dollar earners in a short space of time based on our experiences and skills. Long story short, we were in and became members of this wonderful company, and we had our own insurance business.

This was very new to me, and I had to sit financial exams. We soon made it to the inner circle within Citi-Solutions and moved up the ranks quickly. After two years, the company found out that the UK was not where they needed to be, and made the decision to close shop and head back to the US.

However, they were such an amazing company as they took proper care of everyone. They made calculations and paid everyone who was active some kind of redundancy payment. Some people got paid over £100,000, some got 75k, 50k, 20k, and lower amounts depending on performance. A truly honourable company. Anyway, that was the end of that venture. This was the winter of 2006.

In February of the same year, I married my girlfriend and best friend, Chyna, whom I had been dating for a few years. I was also fortunate enough to have won an incentive trip from Citi-Solutions to Hawaii. We extended the trip and spent a total of 10 days honeymooning in beautiful Hawaii.

That part of me was finally complete. I also packed in my consulting work after 6 years to focus entirely on my speaking and training work, which was beginning to really grow.

GROWING CHARLES KHIRAN INTERNATIONAL

In 2007 my speaking and training business was growing. I was handling some big gigs multi-nationally, including hosting large international conferences with heads of State, heads of corporations like Coca-Cola, Ministers, and other very top government officials were in attendance. The Charles Khiran brand was getting recognised.

Now, because I built a strong reputation as a leader and a people person with the ability to create movements and ignite people, I was always attractive to leaders all over the world who were venturing into the UK to launch their enterprises.

MONAVIE

So, in 2009, some key leaders approached me from America and invited me to help grow the Monavie brand in the UK. I said NO, as I did not want to be distracted. However, they persisted for weeks. Being an entrepreneur at heart and understanding the power of leveraging multiple streams of income, I finally said yes when some multi-million dollar earners began to personally call me with strong propositions.

Monavie achieved the status of the fastest growing multi-level marketing company to achieve a billion dollars in sales in the world. They achieved this incredible feat in less than three and a half years, surpassing companies like Google, Microsoft, or IBM which took 21 years to hit a billion dollars. So, this company was on the move. Fortunately, I could build this business part-time without interrupting my speaking and training business.

Monavie was full of rock stars, big hitters, and flamboyant multi-millionaires with their mansions, boats, Lamborghini's, Ferrari's, Rolls and other exotic cars. They had also cashed in on the nutritional potency of the Acai berry super fruit from Brazil, and became the world's largest consumers. Monavie was able to produce one of the most amazing and tasty liquid nutritional products in a bottle. The products were then sold and distributed through their distribution force of over a million people internationally.

Monavie attracted big names, powerful pastors,

world renowned motivational speakers, and leader-ship gurus. Some of the guys at the top were earning anywhere from $1million dollars a year to $7million dollars. With that kind of money, they could attract almost anybody on board the Monavie ship. I went to work dreaming of replicating this type of success in the UK. I quickly put together a crack team of leaders and we went to work spreading the gospel of super tasty, super healthy and nutritious drinks in exotic bottles.

We achieved quick success. I was invited to the Monavie UK board within 6 months and began to rise through the ranks. At this time, I was personally being coached by my up line leader, the late Darrell Uter-bach. Darrell and I became closer than brothers. He was a Royal Black Diamond, one of the highest ranks in the company, earning between $2-3 million dol-lars annually.

Darrell had one of the biggest hearts. My wife and kids loved him, and my team adored him. However, 2 years into this business, he passed away in his hotel room in South Korea where he had an army of dis-tributors. This sudden and terrible news shook me to my foundations. I cried like a baby.

I remember I was in my hotel room in Nigeria, where I was delivering corporate training for the Cen-tral Bank of Nigeria through my main business, when my wife called me with the very sad news. It was hard to replace Darrell. He sat on the global advisory board for Monavie and he supplied me with high level in-formation from corporate, which informed some of my decisions with my team in the UK.

We attracted really strong powerful ladies and great

men on board and we took the company by storm, creating a powerful reputation within the UK family. Our story and success reached America and even necessitated a visit from top corporate officials from the US to see what we were doing at our meetings. I used the opportunity to recognise some of my top leaders in the presence of these eminent visitors, and got the visitors to hand out certificates of achievement to 30 top performers.

Nothing fires up the human soul like public recognition in front of peers. Anyhow, we did very well and my leaders were able to earn good money. I had some great months as well, sometimes earning up to $10,000 a week, as we were paid commissions weekly.

After Darrell's death, I was mentored for a while by Randy Schroeder, an extremely influential industry veteran and top Black Diamond. Randy had amassed a fortune of over $30 million dollars in his 29 years' experience in the industry and was an incredible trainer.

THE END OF MONAVIE

Two years down the line, the product pricing became an issue along with the limited variety of product options in the UK. It began affecting the business. America had more product choices. The UK was limited to only two products. People were unwilling to pay nearly £40 per bottle for something which lasts only a week. My leaders were beginning to grumble, and the grumbling began to get really loud.

I held regular inspirational meetings, provided emotional support, challenged those who were not pulling their weight, and had serious strategic meetings with my inner circle leaders. Sales were down, and it was getting harder and harder to grow the volume and meet targets. Some of these guys were the same guys who delivered superb results, so it wasn't the fact that they were not able, it was the fact that something was going wrong.

Our meeting numbers were also down. We used to have standing room only and our meeting rooms were packed to the brim. Now, many had gone AWOL (Absent without leave). And as the immortal Jim Rohn (RIP) would say, either the birds had got them, or they had gone into the witness protection program. The people just began to disappear.

One lesson to learn in the sales and marketing environment is this: once the money and buzz goes out of the deal, the crowd usually goes with it. People are notorious for disappearing fast once they smell there is no longer any money. Two years into the deal, I had a crucial meeting with my top leadership and announced we were moving to another opportunity.

Monavie, once the rock star of the industry, began to experience some major challenges, and they eventually were bought out by another fast growing beast in the industry called Jeunesse, who themselves were beginning to break records. Jeunesse swallowed up what was left of Monavie. A lot of the big hitters had moved on to other deals and the rest were absorbed into the Jeunesse family.

NEW OPPORTUNITIES

At this time in late 2011, we were being pitched or approached by various leaders and organisations that could smell blood, hoping my team and I were available in the market. I had the rock solid trust of my leaders and could not just make an easy decision as I was not only deciding for me but for the amazing group of people I had the privilege to lead. So I was very cautious with the various conversations I was having and would share with my top inner circle about 3-5 key individuals.

Then it came down to two opportunities, one representing an American new start-up and fronted by a great American guy, Christopher Hummel, who was instrumental to bringing me on board the Monavie company. He was now with this new outfit and doing quite well. He pressed and pressed, refusing to give up, as he believed I was one of the most effective leaders he had ever met. This was quite flattering, but I had to go with my head and not my heart.

He arranged meetings with the co-founder of the company, who flew to London from the US, to meet with me. I explained that I was really tempted, but I had one other option to look at first before making a decision. At the same time, my old friend of over 20 years, Fred Stege, was launching his own MLM company but with a difference, he was also pitching. Fred had become really successful from when I first knew him over twenty years ago. I mentored him for a while then, but he had since gone on to make a sizable fortune from the industry, building teams of over 100,000 people.

Fred flew in to Stansted airport and we had a meeting at the Radisson hotel next door. We spent many hours discussing the vision. He sold me hard. I told him I would reflect on it, and he flew back home to Sweden.

This was purely an idea at this stage. There was no company as yet, just a vision. It was going to be hard work building structures, developing a range of products, creating a compensation model, ensuring EU & American compliance, corporate staffing, office space, and then the mother of all activities- attracting key leaders on board who are able to drive sales! In the MLM direct selling business, the leaders are worth their weight in gold, they make things happen. So leaders are usually at very high premium because they had the ability to ignite and start movements.

So I got together with two of my inner circle leaders, Itua Aitonje and Charles Emeka, two amazing builders and shared with them the totality of my discussions with Fred. They asked a ton of questions and wanted to be reassured. We got past that stage and they told me they were ready when I was.

ORIGIN CORPORATION

The new company was called 'Origin Corporation' However, the new company did not launch for another 8 months or so as we worked feverishly to put in place the various structures. I had never been involved in an MLM company at this level before. We had literally a blue print and began to work with the blueprint to create a company, we utilised superior technology to create seamless automation in many areas.

There were 3 of us making most of the decisions. Fred, founder and CEO based in Sweden, who had the final say; Maurice van Ophoven, one of the world's best graphic designers and branding experts, based in Norway; and me, based in the UK. Maurice and I headed the field, while Fred and his corporate team looked after corporate affairs.

I took massive action recruiting and sponsoring, attracting leaders and selling the initial vision in preparation for the launch. My key leaders went into overdrive and took the vision to the market with great success.

We were able to attract over 1500 people in the UK and Ireland during the pre-launch phase in preparation for the official company launch. After some teething challenges with the products, comprising of high potency nutritional liquid gels, a superior skin care line, and weight management, we finally launched with great fanfare and expectations.

After a few months, we had to go back to the drawing board and re-strategize. At this time, I had full responsibility and oversight over the UK and Irish markets while still being required to produce as an active distributor.

I threw in maximum commitment, as this was my baby as well, and pulled out all the stops. My nickname for Fred was the 'entreprenerial maverick.' He is an amazing idea generator and does not sleep much. We would discuss our dreams about the business until the early hours of the mornings.

He soon threw an idea at me one day, about a year into the business, and told me he wanted to spend every penny of his fortune in combating malnutrition. He explained that he was extremely unhappy about the needless deaths of millions of kids for something that was such a simple problem to solve.

He then asked me to do some research for him, while he thought of how to integrate this malnutrition fighting cause into the main business. We decided that we would use the fight against malnutrition as our corporate social responsibility (CSR) program.

ORIGIN/UNITE

About 18 months into the business, we finally launched Origin/Unite, as our corporate social responsibility program. We produced a potent product called the 6*59, made up of chewable tablets that tasted like sweets but were loaded with vitamins. Children could consume it by sucking or chewing and it would deliver all the vitamins they needed to help combat malnutrition.

I spent many nights writing the story board, and creating the contents for the Unite website, as we saw the dream begin to take shape. At this time, I was promoted to the position of Vice President for African operations on top of my UK and Ireland responsibilities. I assembled a crack team of leaders to launch the African markets and opened several countries.

I hand-picked key leaders who were working with me in the UK to run the various African markets. We opened Nigeria, Cameroon, and Ghana initially before opening over 10 additional countries. The African leaders were very excited about the 6*59 as they understood by experience the scourge of this dread disease on the lives of the innocent.

The company now had two track processes. Most of Europe wasn't as keen on Origin/Unite. They were focused on the other products, the nutrition, skincare, and weight management lines. However, most of the

African teams and my other teams in South America and Asia were fascinated by the Unite program and the concept of fighting malnutrition.

Then we had a major scoop. Americares, one of the world's leading NGO's, decided to partner with Origin/Unite. They loved the malnutrition combating concept. We signed an MOU with Americares and they began to distribute our donated products around the world to children populations suffering from malnutrition.

I opened up other countries outside my Primary markets. I had oversight over Brazil, Spain, and Bangladesh as I appointed the country leaders for those markets. Fred gave me the freedom to open any country I felt had potential to grow. I received percentages from the turnover from all of my markets.

I ran webinars every Monday night without fail for over 2 years, reaching different parts of the world, so that people who could not physically see me in their distant regions could tune in on their computers and hear me or see me. Even when I was on business trips with my speaking and training business, I would still run the webinars from my hotel room wherever I was in the world. I taught powerful business building strategies and conducted trainings for Africa, UK, Asia, Europe, and on to Brazil on the power of the business.

Soon, my team represented over 60% of the overall company turnover. We generated millions of dollars for the company and we developed tens of thousands of distributors. As with many businesses in this industry, we began to run into some trouble.

After four years, I made the decision to resign from the company. I had thrown everything I had into Origin and I had taken my business as far as I could. I had put out countless fires, developed many powerful leaders, and fought a great fight, but it was time for me to bow out. The vision had become blurred and eyes were taken off the ball.

I was recognised as the face of Origin by many even though it wasn't my company, because I fronted many of the initiatives, announcements, trainings and webinars. Maurice and I had made it to the President's Circle positions, two of the highest ranks in the company, with the attendant and generous remuneration that comes with the positions. Maurice was world number one, and I was number two. Some months I outperformed him and some months he beat me. We were great friends and worked well together as he was my up line.

I also received generous percentages from the turnover of the countries in my care, besides my commissions and bonuses as a distributor. I, of course, signed a non-disclosure agreement as a very senior member of the company and I chose not to go into details with the usual frustrations, hindrances, and challenges experienced at this level.

Origin was a company that was way ahead of its time, a brilliant and clever concept that, however, required huge sums of money to really drive and take it to the levels that it deserved. I am proud that over 50,000 children received treatment for malnutrition around the world. I am proud that some of my top leaders were able to generate incomes of $5000, $7000, $10,000 plus on a monthly basis. And I am proud of the many who were able to earn great part-time incomes of $500, $700, $1000 per month on top of their full-time jobs.

So many people were disappointed when I tendered my resignation. Questions abounded as to why I was leaving. I was pressed for months, but I explained that it was time for me to go, as I did not see any future for me with Origin/Unite anymore. In all truth, I must admit this was one of my greatest regrets, that the company did not become all it was capable of becoming.

We had funding problems and other issues, but it was great while it lasted and the experience was irreplaceable. Sadly, a few months after I left, the company folded up operations. At this time, I would like to pay homage to a few leaders who were instrumental in my and our collective success. These are the individuals I had the privilege of leading. The memory is a bit dim now, as it has been over three years since I left in 2014 February.

Some of my key leaders who helped create our success

• Richard 'the giant' Tchoutezo (RIP), a UK based lawyer who was responsible for the Cameroonian and 9 other markets. An amazing top level performer, Richard unfortunately dropped dead after exercising in 2014.

• Elliott 'the sage' Omose, a successful UK based entrepreneur and manufacturer of the ELkris brand of super oats. Elliott looked after Nigeria

• David Cohen, an amazingly successful entrepreneur who led the Brazilian markets

- Daniel Perez Gomez, who looked after the Spanish markets, a fantastic guy loved by all his people. Dani is now a big time football agent in Spain.

- Apostle Prince Obi, the leading Nigerian distributor

- Dr Sunny Ahonsi, a successful UK based serial entrepreneur, who also looked after our Ghana operations

- Mohammed Harun, a UK successful financial consultant, who ran our Bangladesh operations.

- Itua Aitonje, another UK based giant who did wonders with the business

- Jemima Emmanuel, who created a huge team of dynamic ladies

- Charles Emeka, a professional speaker and trainer and one of the most loyal and committed leaders in my entire team

- Dr Olufemi Osokoya, a practicing GP in the UK, now in Australia, a truly unstoppable guy

- Barrister Julius Nkafu – UK based but in charge of Tanzania and 2 other markets

- Afor Dorcas Kelly – South Africa

- Lady Edith Adesioye - UK

- AbdurRazak Abdul-Azziz - Nigeria

- Janey Ezioba – Nigeria

- Amarachi Ugoji- Nigeria

- Magistrate Edward Forcheh – Cameroon

- Helen Akah – Cameroon

- Nwaobi Orakwe – Nigeria

I struggle to remember so many others right now. However, I want to pay tribute to all the many tens of thousands of people who were part of my organisation over the past 25 years all over the world. Thank you for believing in me and allowing me to lead you. I pray your success will continue in whatever you have gone on to do. You will always have my gratitude as I had the honour of leading such a wonderful group of people like you.

Today I am glad to say I run two very thriving businesses: Charles Khiran International, which handles all my speaking and coaching business, and 3CJ Global my corporate training and consulting company.

We are truly honoured to be highly regarded in the human capital development space as tried and tested professionals who deliver with excellence and precision. I am advisor and coach to politicians and government ministers, ambassadors, high level entrepreneurs, spiritual leaders, royalties, and professionals.

I have personally trained thousands of corporate staff in and out of premises on behalf of many apex organisations internationally. I have been fortunate to have been able to charge up to $65,000 for speaking and coaching engagements, and have developed a reputation as the 'go to guy' in the areas of Leadership, Peak Performance, Customer & Service Excellence, Good Governance, Interpersonal Skills, Communications Skills, Power Public Speaking Skills, and a myriad of other subject matters.

The following chapters contain my thoughts and tips on a host of topics I believe are required for dynamic entrepreneurial success from somebody who has been in the trenches for over two decades with varying degrees of success. See you in the next chapter.

Chapter Two:

What Is An Entrepreneur, And Are You One?

He casts aside his assurance of a 40-hour week, and leaves the safe cover of tenure and security and charges across the perilous field of change and opportunity. If he succeeds, his profit will not come from what he takes from his fellow citizens, but rather from the value they freely place on the gift of his imagination.
–George Gilder

> *ENTREPRENEUR- noun, a person responsible for starting a business or enterprise, taking financial risks in hopes of making a profit. Or somebody responsible for the sustenance or improvement of a business. So this could mean an expansion of a current business, or a new venture creation or self-employment.*

Entrepreneurs are a rare breed of people who are vitally important to the economic health of any country because of their contributions and the opportunities they create for others in terms of jobs. These amazing men and women are risk takers who have made the decision to go it alone, either because they have a unique idea which they want to share with the world, or because they may have been forced into entrepreneurship by default after repeated redundancies due to downsizing from their jobs. This may have influenced their decision to make the leap and take a gamble on themselves into the world of self-employment.

The power of enterprise as a crucial engine for economic growth cannot be underestimated. As a matter of fact, without entrepreneurs, there would be very little innovation, productivity, or jobs being created in the market place anywhere in the world.

For many, they simply got tired of the lack of equal opportunities, or access to the right jobs, due to one reason or the other. There are some countries where innovation flourishes because of the entrepreneurial nature of their citizens according to a survey from the Wharton School of the University of Pennsylvania and BAV Consulting.

The top 5 countries, based on several measurements and specific characteristics, where the majority of entrepreneurs are found: Germany, Japan, USA, UK, and newcomer Switzerland. These are well-established economies that have the resources to support new endeavors both financially and legally. The highest ranked nation, outside of Europe and the Pacific Rim, is the UAE at No. 23.

At No. 32 is South Africa, the first African country to appear on the list, a country that gave the world super players like Elon Musk, the chap who created Paypal, and who has now moved onto space travel and electric cars. He is also the proud manufacturer of the popular Tesla brand of cars. Then there is Tokyo Sexwale, a big player in Oil and Diamonds, who also hosted the SA version of the Apprentice, and mining magnates like Patrice Motsepe.

Brazil came in at No. 38, the first Latin American country to appear on the list. A nation replete with great entrepreneurs, I have a personal knowledge and experience from my dealings with numerous partners from that country over the years.

Big beasts like India and China boast some of the largest concentration of intrepid entrepreneurs, with lightning fast minds and global domination mindsets. Some of the biggest thinkers I have ever come across, besides the Americans, are definitely the Asians.

Another country that cannot be ignored is my native country, Nigeria, boasting some of the smartest people on earth. Many in the country have been forced into self-employment as a means of survival due largely to the paucity of jobs and opportunities for millions of people.

Nigeria is Africa's most populous country and the largest black nation in the world in terms of population and economy. Nigeria also boasts the richest black man in the world, Aliko Dangote, according to Forbes. Aliko Dangote's net worth fluctuates between $14 billion to $22 billion, making him the 23rd richest man in the world.

The Nigerian demographics are also very interesting. According to Wikipedia, Nigerians were at number 7 in terms of mobile phones usage in the world as of 2016. There were 167,000,000 mobile phones in use against a population of approximately 180,000,000.

The other interesting factor is the large proportion of university graduates and a huge population of young under 35's, which accounts for nearly 70% of the 180 million people. They are an extremely energetic and creative people, but many are without gainful employment. For this reason, many are resorting to and being encouraged to take up entrepreneurship. The story is largely the same for many of the African countries.

A lot of these people are forced to seek means of survival, as there is no government social security cushion available. The people must fend for themselves. This has created a dynamic culture of high resiliency and an unstoppable spirit.

Nigerians do not take no for an answer. When you encounter a Nigerian sales person, for example, whether hawking goods on the streets or high level real estate marketer or finance professional, the same spirit flows through them all. This has attracted many international companies flooding in with their various opportunities to a waiting and dynamic populace.

Nigeria also boasts some of the most dynamic billionaires. Besides Dangote, there are other powerful super-entrepreneurs like Tony Elumelu, one of Africa's most revered business leaders, worth about $1 billion; Mike Adenuga, worth over $9.9 billion according to Forbes; Folorunsho Alakija, the first female billionaire in Nigeria and one of the top 3 richest black women in the world. She made her money from fashion and oil.

There are four main types of entrepreneurs, here are some:

• *Manufacturing entrepreneurs*, whose chief domain is identifying the needs of consumers and sourcing and identifying products to satisfy or meet those needs.

• *Technology entrepreneurs*, who essentially take a technology idea and marry it to high potential commercial opportunities. They also seek out the right resources, like talent and capital, and then identify how to exploit the idea through marketing for potential rapid growth.

• *Private entrepreneurs*, those individuals who set up a business and bear the full risk of what happens to it. The idea and innovation for the business come primarily from the entrepreneur's efforts to solve social and economic problems.

• *Agricultural entrepreneurs*, who are mainly farmers concerned with the cultivating and the marketing of agricultural produce to meet the food needs of the population.

SO DO YOU HAVE WHAT IT TAKES?

> *"In the middle of difficulty lies opportunity" – Albert Einstein*

We regularly read and hear about some highly inspirational entrepreneurial figures, many of whom went from rags to staggering riches like Richard Branson of Virgin, Larry Ellison of Oracle, Oprah Winfrey, the Queen of media, Jeff Bezos of Amazon, or the richest man in Asia, Li Ka-Shing. The world has also seen a rapid rise in new young billionaires largely due to the current digital age utilising the power of information, knowledge, and technology.

This has introduced us to young entrepreneurial icons like Facebook founder, Mark Zuckerberg; Snapchat founder, Evan Spiegel; and Robotics firm founder, Frank Wang; and many others.

However, before you make the decision to take the plunge into entrepreneurship, you have to ask yourself the important question: Have I got what it takes to succeed as an entrepreneur?

Why? Because entrepreneurship is not for the faint hearted, due largely to the attendant risks and very high failure rates involved. The commercial landscape is littered with the carcasses of failed businesses. Entrepreneurship will take everything you have got. The World Economic Forum puts the failure rate at about 90%. That is a staggering rate of businesses and ventures that do not make it.

The huge failure rates are also compounded by the fact that so many are forced into entrepreneurship without proper preparation, mentorship, or apprenticeship. Many have never held proper jobs, and have never been in corporate environments where they possibly would have learnt discipline and best practices.

And for those who have come out of the corporate environment, many are so used to regimented regimes, when to go for lunch break, start work, and finish work, or when to go for their vacations. All of these things are planned for them by the Human Resources department.

A lot of these ex-corporate types have not learnt how to employ themselves and be their own bosses. For others, their personal habits are sabotaging their potential for success, whether due to poor interpersonal skills in terms of attitudes and behaviour, professionalism, communications skills, verbal and listening skills, or leadership.

The crucial question to ask yet again is: Do you have what it takes to make it as an entrepreneur?

Let us now look at some characteristics, traits, and work ethics possessed by successful entrepreneurs. You do not have to possess them all. However, you should possess a high proportion.

These are a general guide and are not exhaustive, which means you can still succeed even without some of these, however your chances will be more enhanced by the possession of a lot of these.

• *Attitude:* Self-employment requires certain skills, abilities and knowledge; but most of all – ATTITUDE (mindset). This is the first prerequisite for winning in business. Your attitude must be that of a winner! The right ATTITUDE will definitely take you to the top.

• *Passion:* Are you passionate about the business idea and full of enthusiasm for it?

• *Optimism:* Do you have the ability to see problems and challenges as opportunities?

• *Visionary*: This is the ability to see in your mind's eye what can be, and then going to work to bring it into reality, plus never being satisfied with the status quo.

• *Curious:* Are you curious and do you question everything?

• *Decisive:* Are you quick to make decisions, and slow to change your mind having decided?

• *Competitive:* Most entrepreneurs understand ambitious and harmonious rivalry, do you?

• *Spongers:* Entrepreneurs have an insatiable thirst for knowledge, and they constantly apply CANEI (continuous and never ending improvement)

• *Flexible:* Entrepreneurs are responsive to change and know how to set their sails.

• *Goal-setting:* Entrepreneurs are consummate goal setters. They are always measuring their progress and responding accordingly. They set 1, 3, 5, and 10 year goals, and work towards the goals.

• *Sensory Acuity:* They have sharp perceptions and practice intelligent objectivity.

- *Self-Motivated:* They are driven by their desire to give the world their gift, and they know if it is to be, it is going to be up to them. They do not wait for people to come along to fire them up, they have an internal thermometer to regulate their own temperature.

- *Courageous:* Entrepreneurs take action in spite of their fears. They understand courage is not the absence of fear, but it is the ability to take action regardless of the fear.

- *Persistence:* They possess this quality of never giving up, and staying with it until the end.

- *Risk Taking:* Entrepreneurs are risk takers. They take intelligent and calculated risks. They are not afraid to swim in uncharted waters in order to discover new horizons.

- *Frugal:* They are careful with money. They dislike wastefulness. They appreciate what things cost and the value of money to their business.

- *Loners:* Many entrepreneurs are loners, preferring to work alone as opposed to working in teams. Many super-entrepreneurs are actually introverts, such as Larry Page of Google and Zuckerberg of Facebook. Of course, you don't need to be an introvert to succeed as an entrepreneur. However, even the extroverts have large moments of loneliness as they work to make their dream succeed.

- *Professional:* Entrepreneurs tend to be very professional in terms of their approach and attitude to work.

- *High Energy:* They are highly driven people and exert high energy in pursuit of their dreams, many times working an average of 12 hour days.

- *Displayed early entrepreneurial signs:* Many entrepreneurs started earning money at a very early age by selling things, whether it was sweets, shirts, concert tickets at school, babysitting, washing cars, mowing the lawn, buying and fixing bikes, buying cars and then selling them, etc.

- *College dropout:* Many entrepreneurs struggle to fit in with the crowd or with traditional education. Many ditched contemporary education completely and took a risk on themselves. Branson, Gates, CNN's Ted Turner, and so many others, dropped out of high school or college.

- *Black sheep:* Many are also perceived as the black sheep in the family, with everyone secretly thinking they won't amount to much. They usually become the most successful in the family as they run with their dreams.

- *Dislikes authority:* The other thing I found out about potential entrepreneurs, is that they dislike authority figures and a 9-5 routine. They do not like having to answer to so-called bosses. As a matter of fact, they thrive in uncertainties and treasure their freedom and independence.

Now compare the above list with yours and see how many ticks you have. This should give you a good indication of whether or not you are cut out to be an entrepreneur. The allure is very strong. If, however, you have decided you have what it takes, then launch out and throw everything you have got into it.

Finally, go make a success of it. Who knows? We may be talking or reading about you very soon!

Chapter Three:

Developing A CCMP Of Your Desire

"When you want to succeed as much as you want to breathe, then you will be successful"
– *Eric Thomas*

It is interesting to observe that once a person has firmly made up his mind to achieve a specific goal or travel in a particular direction, then everything comes along to try to dissuade them or interrupt them from achieving it. These can come in various guises.

It may come as well-meaning friends with great advice for you. It may be well-intentioned people bringing you the hottest opportunity since the invention of the internet, and telling you how you are going to become the next millionaire if you say yes quickly.

I have had my fair share of those over the years. Some are genuinely great opportunities. Some people have actually become very wealthy from some of these opportunities. My focus is not to disparage the opportunities these good people bring to your attention.

However, the moment you make a firm decision to go in a particular direction, then every obstacle will be thrown in front of you to stop you. One of the hardest things you will ever do is to make a decision for your life's direction. So many struggle to find out what they were put here on planet Earth to accomplish or do. In other words, the discovery of their purpose.

The moment you discover what you were truly put on the earth to do, half the battle is over. There is a great medical metaphor that says a 'proper diagnosis is half the cure'. That is so true. Once you can properly diagnose the ailment, then you will know where to direct the appropriate treatment.

The big challenge is when the ailment, condition, or disease cannot be diagnosed. Then the medical professionals will use you as an experiment as they throw everything at you, hoping one of the treatments may just do the job.

The same dictum applies with your purpose or life's direction. This is to say, when you have a firm idea of your purpose, then it makes so much sense to launch your business or enterprise in line with your purpose.

Using myself as an example, I have gifts in the areas of high impact speaking, leadership development, and training. I have always been a person who attracts people seeking answers about different things and questions about life. So, it was a very natural predilection to launch a business offering training, coaching, speaking, and consulting. I use my gifts and skills to provide comfort to stressed and weary people seeking solutions. I help people who want to be more effective in their lives, business or careers.

What if you ask me to launch a business in oil & gas, mining, hedge funds, accounting, electronics, jewellery making, solar energy, graphic Design, for example? It is quite possible that I could retrain to operate some of the above. However, I have to ensure I have a passion and an understanding of it to have any hope of succeeding.

The other option is to hire people to run it for me, of course. However, the point I am making here is to go for a business where you have natural gifts and passion. That way, you have a flow and love for what you do. What many people tend to do is to first focus on where they think the money is by asking what business will bring in the most money.

You see, we were all created with different gifts, strengths, and passions. That simply means we all have different things that attract us. By pursuing our individual passions, we give the world the beauty and variety of our collective best.

When you operate an enterprise in the areas of your passions and gifts, then it doesn't seem to be like a job anymore, it becomes work.

Here is what work will do for you:

-   Work is something that allows you to birth your innate gifts and talents.

-   Work allows you to give expression to the divine in you.

-   Work gives you maximum satisfaction.

-   Work won't allow you to get bored, for it was what you were put on earth to do.

-   Work allows your full potential to be unleashed.

-   Work will allow you to innovate naturally, because the more you are in love with what you do, the more inspiration and flow occurs to help you think outside the box

LINUS'S STORY

I was attracted to my new friend the highly successful social entrepreneur and leadership change agent, Linus Okorie, because of the great work his organisation does in Africa. I was in Abuja, the capital of Nigeria, late 2016. I was preparing to return back to London early the next morning.

Since I could not sleep, I decided to post some images on Facebook of the high profile event I had just facilitated for the Nigeria Petroleum Minister Emmanuel Ibe Kachikwu's books launch (3 books) in Abuja. Linus saw the details on Facebook and messaged me immediately from Dubai, where he was attending a program late in the night.

I recognised his name and we had a brief conversation on Messenger. We have since become well acquainted and are planning various strategic collaborations. His story captivated me and it sings loudly of the power of vision and unwavering focus (CCMP). Here is Linus story in his own words:

THE POWER OF FOCUS:

I lost my father at a very young age. Before his death, he made my mother promise to do everything in her power to make sure I got an education. She did her best, ensuring I got into one of the best secondary schools in Nigeria at the time, Government Secondary School, Owerri, Imo State.

My mother did not have a lot of money, but did everything in her power to ensure I could pay my fees, including selling her jewellery and borrowing money. The other necessities I needed for life in a boarding school, I provided for myself. I also had a sense that I was destined for greatness.

My first expression of leadership and leadership development was in the Secondary school when I nursed the quiet ambition to become the Senior Prefect of the school. This was the highest student leadership position in any secondary school. I had oppositions and discouragement from other pupils, but I was dedicated to the cause and worked hard to be seen as the exemplary senior student and role model for younger students. It worked!

I was announced as senior prefect of the institution in 1995 and my leadership style endeared me to many, staff and students alike. I was passionate about leadership.

As the Senior Prefect of the school, I was actively involved in hosting the alumni meetings. These were meetings of men who had passed through the school, and were usually held in the school premises.

These meetings gave me the opportunity to network with older men who had become successful in their various spheres of influence. I got to know many of them on a personal basis and was even invited over to their homes for holidays.

After my secondary education, I came to another crossroad. I needed money to progress to university, but had none. My mother had done her best and could not do much any longer. My vision was absolutely clear. I knew I would surely attend university, but had no idea how it would happen.

My focus was so strong that I reached out to some of the older men who had attended my school, the Old Boys. I called almost all of the people in the Old Boys' Association directory to request support. It was challenging, but I was so passionate and focused that I got all the support I needed.

During this period of waiting and working to gain admission into the university, I decided to attend a Bible School, the Word Of Faith Bible Institute (WOF-BI), founded by the legendary Dr. David Oyedepo. I came across the story of Nehemiah, who built his country in spite of difficult oppositions. I wept for the state of my country, Nigeria, and for Africa.

I just wanted to import the kind of leadership Nehemiah had promoted to Nigeria and the rest of Africa. That singular experience became the game changer and focus of my life.

I began to ask tough and soul searching questions as to why Nigeria was in its current state. Why has it remained underdeveloped despite the huge and enviable human and mineral resources she is blessed with?

I discovered that there was a paucity of visionary and quality leadership, not just in government but also in the spheres of business, education, family, media, and across other sectors.

The search for answers to these questions led to the birth of Guardians of the Nation International (GOT-NI) at the age of 19. I had created an organization at the same time while I was searching for sponsorship to get through university. What a heavy burden this was, but I was single minded and focused.

Armed with the discovery of my new-found life's assignment, vision, and mandate, my quest for knowledge, wisdom and insight began. I began to ask myself questions like "What can I do to remedy the situation of Nigeria?" and "What role can I play?"

A heavy beam of light illuminated my soul. I had a eureka moment and consequently the purpose of my existence became clear and defined – to raise a generation of leaders who would serve with passion, integrity and excellence, beginning with Nigeria.

I proceeded to Imo State University, where I studied History and International Relations. While at university, I started mobilizing groups of young people who bought into the vision of grooming the next generation of leaders for Nigeria.

We started leadership campaigns using the GOT-NI brand with a focus in nurturing various categories of young people under forty years of age, into transformational leaders who would impact positively the various sectors of the society and economy in the immediate future.

This movement, which started as a student-driven mandate, has grown to cities and countries across the world today.

At that time, all I could see were possibilities. I could see the possibility of a transformed and prosperous nation, blessed with men and women of honour, vision, integrity, service, and courage as her leaders and followers. I communicated this vision to everyone who cared to listen.

The vision seemed out of scope at the time and so there were lots of mockers. Some people could not understand the so-called leadership capital development 'gospel' that I was pioneering. My focus and commitment deepened. I kept the mental picture (CCMP) of what was to be accomplished and drove myself beyond the limits.

My dream was to see a transformed Nigeria, able to export leadership capital to other nations of the world. My quest continued while as a fresh undergraduate, and I resolved to express it. I determined to become the Student Union Government President and, in spite of obvious challenges towards becoming the first elected president, my vision and passion were stronger than the obstacles in my way.

I eventually emerged as the first elected Student Union Government President of Imo state University in 1998. My administration witnessed visionary leadership as a result of my grooming to many other leaders working with me. Part of my desire was to set the STAR HOUSE, which was to serve as the administrative hub, and secretariat of the Student Union that we built as a team.

The reality was unprecedented. My position as Student Union Government president offered me great opportunities to further nurture, express, and ultimately improve my leadership abilities.

Years after graduation, in my quest to fully establish Guardians of the Nation International (GOTNI), we registered it with the Corporate Affairs Commission in 2004, and it assumed a legal status as a non-profit organisation.

For more than two decades now, GOTNI has imparted and groomed thousands of Nigerians into transformational leaders who are making a difference in their spheres in Nigeria, throughout Africa, and across the world through ground-breaking mindset revolutionary programmes. Our brands for leadership outreach include Nigeria Youth Leadership and Economic Summits, Emerging Leaders Conferences, Leadership Clinic sessions with mentors, Young Women Leadership Programmes, National Youth Service Corps (NYSC) Programmes, Mission to Schools programmes, and Leaders Forum weekly sessions, amongst other partnerships through which we have impacted youths.

Not to forget our media outreaches and continuous social media drive through which we have reached even more people with the possibilities of being servant leaders for Nigeria's development. Steadily, we are building a new generation of leaders for Africa.

With the establishment of the GOTNI Leadership Centre Phase 1 in Abuja, we are set to revolutionise leadership development in Nigeria, with a permanent Leadership Centre to be cited in 7-hectares of land overlooking the Oguta Lake, in Imo state. We look forward to expanding our operations across the world.

This hub will be established as the first ever African Leadership Centre in Imo state Nigeria. It will serve as the Pan African Leadership Development Institute which will train, nurture and groom leaders and aspiring leaders with the vision of exporting exemplary leadership from Nigeria to other parts of the world. Driven by this great vision, I have acquired a Master's Degree in Organizational Leadership from Regent University in the USA, attended many leadership short courses in institutions around the world, including the Kennedy School of Government at Harvard University.

I have also received various fellowships around the world including IVLP from the United States Government. I have also had the honour of hosting some of the best names in the world on leadership development in Nigeria, from Prof. John Adair, Dr. Myles Munroe (RIP), Prof. John Keenam, Dr. George C. Fraser, and many more. This can only be God's grace and the unrelenting capacity to pursue my dream.

These three things have kept me on track. Firstly, the power of vision and focus. Secondly, the power of perseverance and consistency. Third, the power of delayed gratification.

I love to always say "if a man does not have a purpose for waking up, sleeping becomes interesting." Create your own vision that you can feel, touch, and get excitement and passion from, which will enable you leave your comfort zone consistently to pursue it.

Most of the time only you can see, feel, and touch your vision. Keeping it alive requires a great sense of focus and the art of single mindedness. I made up my mind to make the dream happen.

I saw today "yesterday". I paid the price, and now I am enjoying the fruits of a social entrepreneur. while I am not yet where I want to be, I have definitely made huge strides toward an uncommon future.

THE PRINCIPLE OF FOCUS

Linus' incredible story demonstrates powerfully what CCMP stands for; a clear, concise mental picture. Anyone who has ever attained significant success in business, sports, entertainment, the professions, or in life must possess a CCMP. This is also known as the principle of focus. It is impossible to attain mastery in anything without this principle.

This principle derives its power from your ability to combine all your mental and emotional faculties, and channel them through concentration toward achieving a definite goal or objective, or your life's purpose.

When you bring the might of your faculties and direct them without distraction to whatever you desire to achieve, then the world begins to make way for you.

Every single person who comes into your employ will be focused on the same objectives. The synergistic effect of all the mind's powers concentrated in the spirit of harmony, will begin to generate extraordinary results. In today's world, people are interested in specialization or expertise, and not in generalities. Which means whatever you do, aim to be the very best you are capable of being in that field of endeavour or discipline.

Imagine if you have been told you are in danger of losing your eye or limb. You are told there is a doctor who treats everything and there is an eye specialist who is an expert purely on eyes. Which one will you have more confidence in when your precious eye is at stake? Of course your choice will obviously be for the eye specialist because you don't want anyone experimenting with your eyes.

That is the same aphorism in business. Make yourself known and recognised as somebody or a business who delivers superior quality and results in a particular area of skill and expertise. That is what discerning customers seek.

Now when it comes to the accumulation of knowledge, we should go all out and acquire it, as the late billionaire Andrew Carnegie advises. However, when it comes to the execution and expression of that knowledge, we should concentrate it on the attainment of a definite major purpose. This essentially means a specialisation or expertise in an area.

I know so many people who are involved in several businesses or opportunities, and they usually quote Henry Ford or Robert Kiyosaki as their inspiration. They explain the idea of multiple streams of income. There is no real problem with that, if you want to be an average Joe. If you want to rule your space and dominate your niche, you can't be a generalist. You have to become a meaningful specific, an expert, or a specialist.

Look at all the greats around you from Ronaldo the soccer star, to the boxing sensation Anthony Joshua, to Oprah, Anthony Robbins, Les Brown, Bill Gates, Mark Zuckerberg, and all the other endless lists of highly successful people. You will find this principle at the core of their success – intense focus in an area.

They can be investors, of course, in lots of different things, but they are uniquely known for something. For every meaningful specific person, their time is spent on the identification of their life's purpose.

Once they find it, all their energy and strength is now focused on the attainment of that major life's purpose. Guess what? It will attract all the success and money you crave. So, the lesson here is not to focus on the money, but the focus must be on the purpose, and it will attract the money as you develop expertise and high value.

7 KEYS TO APPLYING YOUR CCMP

1.   Lock in and define your clear, concise mental picture of what you want. What is the desire for your life? What is your life's purpose? What would you like to achieve or be known for? How do you want to contribute value to the world?

The majority of people do not actually know what they want. As a speaker, coach, and trainer I see this all the time. You must work on this important part of knowing what you really want. You may start with something initially for survival, or to make ends meet, but sooner or later your mind will begin to move in the direction of your purpose.

2.   Once you know what you want, determine to establish your enterprise in the area or areas/s of your CCMP. You already possess the gifts, strengths, and passions in this particular area. All that remains is to develop the requisite skills or dexterity required for success.

3.   Refuse to be distracted by all the different opportunities people bring to you. By all means, evaluate some of them and see if it fits with your direction of travel. If it doesn't, let it go as it will only be a distraction. Believe me, I have been there many times. The old maxim of a 'Jack or Jill of all trades, and expert in none' comes to mind.

4.   Next, focus without distraction in learning all you can about your business. Even though you have natural passions and gifts in this area, you will still need to develop expertise. Read industry journals, follow and investigate the businesses that stand out, check out your highly successful competitor's websites and see what is new. All these are important while you are positioning yourself in your niche.

5.   Attend courses, seminars, trainings, and focus on acquiring knowledge, especially knowledge to market more successfully and attract clients and customers.

6.   Find a coach or a mentor you admire to help you raise your game.

7.   Go for mastery. To attain mastery, you need diligence. Diligence is conscientiousness, thoroughness, and meticulousness. It is essentially bringing excellence and quality to what you do. Determine to use your passion, diligence, enthusiasm, knowledge, and determination to be the best you are capable of becoming. This will impact what you do and bring you the success you desire and deserve.

Finally, let me leave you with a quote from Robert Collier, the 20th Century American author. He said "The great successful men and women of the world have used their imagination...They think ahead and create their mental picture in all its details, filling in here, adding a little there, altering this a bit and that a bit, but steadily building, steadily building"

Chapter Four:

Making The Decision And Taking Your Dream To The World

> "Work hard in silence. Let your success make the noise"
> -*Frank Ocean*

The iconic Sir Richard Branson advised that the key to success is intention! To get us on the way in this chapter, let us get some sage advice from the iconic 18th Century German writer Wolfgang Von Goethe, the multi-talented German writer:

"There is one elementary truth, the ignorance of which kills countless ideas and splendid plans. That the moment one definitely commits oneself, providence moves, too. All sorts of things occur to help one that would never otherwise have occurred. A whole stream of events issues from the decision, rising in one's favour. All matter of unforeseen incidents and meetings and material assistance which no man could have dreamed would have come his way. Are you in earnest? Seize this very minute. What you can do or dream you can, begin it. Boldness has genius, power and magic in it. Begin it now! Only engage and the mind grows heated. Begin it and the work will be completed"

There are various routes you can embark on your entrepreneurial journey. The key questions to ask are, "What is your dream or vision for your life? What have you been dreaming of that you would like to present to the world? What is that unique idea, invention or opportunity you believe you can put your signature on?"

Napoleon Hill, author of one of the biggest selling books in history, 'Think & Grow Rich,' explained the concept of two types of vision as taught by Andrew Carnegie. So your vision or idea will either be one of two types of creativity. It will either be a Creative Vision, or it will be a Synthetic Vision.

Now what is the difference?

Creative Visions are rarer, revolutionary, new ideas

or concepts never before seen or experienced. Creative visions can be birthed by the free and fearless use of your imagination. This is where you bring a never before seen idea, product or concept to the market. Examples of creative visions include; the telephone, the internet, airplane, motorcar, electricity, vaccines, Social Media, etc. These are never before seen in the world.

The second types are Synthetic Visions. These are more evolutionary, as opposed to revolutionary. These types of visions are more common. Here you take an existing idea, product, or concept, and you improve it. For example, different restaurants or fast food chains, personal computers, different brand of cars, newer versions of social media, the Uber taxi revolution, weight management, charitable organisations, franchises, Airbnb, and the list is endless.

Below is a story of a great friend of mine Titilola, and how she stumbled upon her own entrepreneurial journey. Titi was born into one of the wealthiest families in the whole of Africa, however, she is a very humble and simple lady, carving a niche for herself without the aid of her family fortune. Below is her story in her own words:

TITILOLA MADEDOR'S STORY

When asked when and how my entrepreneurial journey began, I would have to say at birth, but through no means of my own. Being born to parents who are both strong business-minded individuals gave me a tremendous advantage towards realizing all my business goals and dreams. I believe that I have the inbuilt DNA to succeed and failure is just not an option.

I left Nigeria, my country of birth, at the age of 8 and attended a Swiss school in the middle of nowhere in a village called Villar. La Garenne, my elementary school, was and is a chalet that has about 50 students enrolled at any given year. Being the brilliant minded person that I am, I became fluent in French in 6 months, although I believe it had more to do with the fact that the school was isolated and was in the French speaking part of Switzerland.

Most of my primary and secondary education was in Switzerland, and I believe that it set the platform for who I am today. My years in Switzerland were some of the best years of my life, not for my academic endeavours, but because I cultivated the best and most lasting friendships that would hopefully last a life time.

Growing up with members of the world's elite afforded me the mind-set and exposure that has been incomparable to any other time or place since. To this day, there is no country in the world I may choose to visit where I do not have a friend I went to school with living.

Although I should have gone to school to study business or something along those lines, I succumbed to the pressure of my African parents, who wanted their children to be either doctors or lawyers. I got my first degree in Biochemistry at the University of Buckingham in the UK. That not being enough, I went to medical school at Howard University in Washington D.C.) for about 2 years before I got the revelation that this was not really what I wanted to do.

After deciding it was time to start living my life for myself, much to my parent's displeasure, and with much inner struggle, I left medical school. I decided I still liked helping people, but I wanted to do it my own way. I started learning about alternative/holistic medicine, and I found an area I felt suited my temperament while allowing me to remain true to myself.

Within a year or so of learning about different modalities of alternative medicine, I decided to buy and takeover an existing health and wellness center in Virgina, USA. That was truly the start of my journey to becoming an entrepreneur.

Considering that my parents were business owners, there was no doubt in my mind that this was the way to go. I just knew that working for someone else was not for me, not because I thought it was beneath me, but because I was just following the example that had been set for me.

The 6-month period I tried working for an employer in a health and wellness center proved that I was not meant to work for somebody else, as every time I took initiative, it seemed to threaten the owner of the business.

When I finally started my own health and wellness business, I ran it for about 6 years before I decided to move back to Nigeria permanently. At the time I returned home, I had lived in different countries for about 30 years.

I felt it was time for me to go back home. My parents were getting on in age and I was missing out on significant family events. The decision to move back home was the best decision for me, as it positioned me to line up with my calling. I believe when a person lines up with their calling, things that seem impossible fall into place almost like a person taking their next breath without conscious thought.

Being an entrepreneur means that you will start, and start over, several times with various projects until you find a fit. You will not rest, you will not sleep, and you will not know peace until you find what you are destined to do. You will try this project or that one in the hope that you get there.

I believe that is exactly what happened to me. I have a million and one ideas, some of them really great ideas, going through my head at all times. Some of these ideas I have tried with all the passion in the world, believing that maybe, just maybe this is what I am meant to do. It is not until you find your fit or calling that it all comes together and you just know that that particular project/goal or job is what you are destined to do.

I believe I stumbled upon my calling accidentally. In the process of trying to start up one of my many projects, I was searching for land to buy in the highly sought after and fast developing Ibeju-Lekki area of Lagos state to build a factory. I came across some people who introduced me to some family/land owners from whom I got some land.

I met these Land Owners and found favour with them and got into the land business with them. I was again introduced to some other family/Land Owners that I transacted some more business with and that is how I have been able to amass significant land ownership, and got into the Real Estate business.

My journey in the Real Estate business has just started. Our company Motik Consulting Ltd. has just started taking baby steps, but our vision is tremendous. Real Estate in Lagos is an area that is untapped and, if done right, can greatly impact our community for the good. We have and are continuing to position ourselves to be a well-known brand in Real Estate in the next decade or so.

RESEARCHING YOUR IDEAS

Once you decide on your idea or opportunity, you have to test it and be sold out completely on it. This could be an invention, a concept, product, or existing opportunity like buying a franchise, launching a technology or online business, or starting an MLM business.

There are many well-tested business options out there that you could choose. Real estate has been incredibly successful for many. Brick & Mortar businesses have created some extremely wealthy people around the world, and continue to do so. You just cannot beat owning land and property.

I have good friends who are making fortunes from this industry and the list is growing. There are so many cities around the world from very developed to developing where property investment and ownership still reigns supreme.

Online retail business

People are finding entrepreneurial success from all types of business opportunities. One of the fast emerging option for some is online and internet marketing fuelled by excellent technology like cloud-based storage options, high powered smart phones, tablets, and, of course, laptops. There is a big rise in internet or online entrepreneurs from all over the world providing excellent and niche services, and generating handsome profits from their online enterprises.

There are so many who are deriving great satisfaction working from home and marketing digital products online. Many of these individuals are making their fortunes from this fast emerging option with a great future. This is partly due to the fact that more and more of us are spending a lot of time online seeking various solutions and options.

Further, the small start-up cost involved is a great attraction, plus the global reach for the entrepreneurs is another big plus. According to data from the US, the ecommerce and online retail is estimated at approximately $200 billion dollars and projected to grow by 15% annually. One of the reasons for this incredible success is the power and advancement of technology.

The other major plus driving this huge growth is the simplicity and options of payment and collection. PayPal has been a life saver for many, offering online payment options, and also a simple process of collecting your money from customers from different parts of the world. It's been a true game changer!

Another reason for some entrepreneurial successes in online retailing is smart partnership with giants like Amazon, eBay or Alibaba. The entrepreneurs pay a commission to use the platforms and storage facilities of some of these behemoths, and their products are not only sold on these sites, but they also provide cost effective and superior delivery options and customer service too. This has been a true win-win for the entrepreneurs, but at a cost obviously.

Franchises

A lot of people have found buying a franchise as an entrepreneurial option. Franchises did not really come into their own until about 40-50 years ago, as people began to take it a bit more seriously. It has now been successfully proven over the decades as a viable form of business after initially undergoing a very difficult period in order to be accepted as legitimate form of business.

A lot of them require on average from $15,000 - $50,000 in fees for the smaller options, however these do not usually include the costs of opening or operating the business, which could skyrocket to upwards of hundreds of thousands of dollars or millions, depending on the type of franchise. Franchises offer a turn-key opportunity, or a ready-made business model, which comes along with training, guidance and support.

Franchises have also been experiencing very strong jobs growth in recent years, averaging 2.6% annually, which is nearly 20% higher than traditional businesses according to the IFA (International Franchising Association) 2016 report.

However, there are many factors to consider and also heavy risks involved. I have met a few franchise owners over the years who have lost heavily. I have also met some who have become multi-millionaires. You must ensure you look closely at the franchise opportunity and, most importantly, decide whether this style of business suits your personality.

Some of the very well-known and established franchise brands include the following:

- Mcdonald's
- KFC
- Burger King
- Subway
- Hertz
- Pizza Hut
- Marriott International
- Hilton Hotels & Resorts
- Re/max
- Kumon
- Dunkin Donuts
- Baskin Robbins
- Century 21
- Europecar
- TGI Fridays
- Domino Pizza
- Costa Coffee
- Starbucks
- ServiceMaster Clean

- Intercontinental Hotels Group

- Krispy Kreme Doughnut

Multi-Level Marketing

Another very popular entrepreneurial option millions of people have taken advantage of is Multi-Level Marketing because of the low start-up costs. As a matter of fact, it has been firmly established that MLM has created more millionaires than any other industry over the past 50 years. In Robert Kiyosaki's book 'Business of the 21st Century', he also made mention of this fact too.

America, Japan, Europe, Asia, and Africa, in that order, boasts multiplied tens of thousands who have made their fortunes from the MLM industry, with America and Japan probably boasting the most millionaires.

I personally enjoyed great success in this industry before launching my professional speaking, coaching, and corporate training business. I spent over 18 years actively building my MLM organisations with 5 separate companies. I achieved top of the table with two of the companies, making it to the very top and developing a distributor base of nearly 40,000 entrepreneurs in my business.

I have some close friends and mentors from this industry. Some of these individuals earn an average of $500,000 - $4million dollars (US) annually. These individuals live like rock stars, with their mansions, boats, exotic cars etc. Some of them are also the biggest contributors to good causes I know.

What is exciting about this particular industry is what you become in the process of building your MLM business. You get to go through intense personal development and leadership development training in order to succeed. This has been termed the regular people's franchise because of the low start-up costs associated with it as opposed to the requirements of traditional business.

You could actually launch your own entrepreneurial business in the MLM industry with as little as $150 - $1,500 to purchase some initial products to start your business, and have the potential to earn as much as somebody who owns a hotel or a large McDonald's franchise.

As opposed to investing large upfront costs, you actually invest real sweat equity, making up in effort what you lack in upfront money investment. MLM will also teach you vital life skills in terms of understanding human behaviour, leadership & interpersonal skills, sales skills, communication skills, learning how to handle rejection, tenacity and perseverance, and so many other life transforming skills.

Let's not also forget the fun part. There is a lot of fun socialising with MLM, as it is a people's business, and many people join because of the travel to exotic locations, conventions and other events associated with it.

The biggest issue many people have with this industry is the perceived negativity, due largely to some who failed to make a success of it, and consequently talk it down. Should you be attracted to this form of business, it is critical to select the right company, as there are some notorious and illegal companies masquerading as genuine MLM companies. Here again, there are pros and cons with selecting.

Some of the older and more established companies do not pay as much as most of the newer ones. However, the risk of failure associated with the newer ones are very high. So you have to carefully select using some key criteria. Do you want to go for long term stability and earn a bit less, or would you take a gamble with the newer operators where there is the potential to make more money available in the compensation plan, but it could be risky?

With newer companies, as long as you are the driven leader type, you could benefit from 'first mover advantage' which is essentially early positioning within the company's hierarchical structure before everyone starts flooding in. This will only be a benefit as long as you are prepared to take massive action, or else somebody who joins years later could easily overtake you in income and rank by exercising dynamic building skills.

On the other hand, there are newer companies that went on to create many millionaires and succeeded in magnificent fashion. If the attraction of a new company is there for you, I would advise you to ensure the company is well-funded, or has a more established powerful company behind it, because MLM companies need plenty of money to keep them well lubricated.

Next thing to look for is the products or services that most appeal to you. I found companies with actual physical products to be more stable and successful overall. These days, anything from cleaning products, super nutritionals, superior skincare, weight management, insurance, investments, travel, make up, fashion, and jewellery and so many other products are marketed through many of the companies.

Here is a list of some of the more dominant, powerful, and successful companies. Some of these are multi-billion dollar companies and are still experiencing tremendous growth. The potential to truly succeed is very strong.

In no particular order:

- Herballife
- Avon
- Jeunesse
- Amway
- Nu Skin
- Primerica
- Juice Plus
- Oriflame
- Forever Living
- Usana
- Isagenix
- ACN
- Nerium

- Natures Sunshine
- Mannatech
- Zija
- Ariix
- Tiens
- Longrich
- Scentsy
- World Ventures
- Market America
- Mary Kay
- Vorwerk
- Tupperware
- Morinda (Tahitian Noni)
- Arbonne
- Ambit Energy
- Forever Green-FgXpress
- Global Wealth Trade
- Melaleuca
- Shaklee
- Visalus
- Xango

These are just a few. There are literally hundreds of companies, so do your research and see which ones you truly love. Then, roll up your sleeves and go to work. You just may have your dreams become reality.

I have met some incredibly successful individuals who have not only changed the lives of their friends and family members, but also their community and society, through their entrepreneurial success. For an example of the types of individuals drawn into the MLM industry, here is the story of my very good friend and the huge successes he recorded by going all out.

FRED PASCAL STEGE'S STORY

My good friend and former business partner, Fred P. Stege, was born "Fredrick Pascal Stege Beaufort" but prefers to be called Fred. He is one of the big success stories from the MLM industry. He is a Dutch citizen and a descendant of one of Europe's oldest families.

He now makes his home by the water and the great bridge in beautiful Malmo, Sweden overlooking Copenhagen. When not found playing his beloved game of golf, he can be found in his other favourite hideout in Mallorca, Spain, where he owns a spectacular mansion overlooking the Andratx habour.

Fred could also be found busy crisscrossing the globe with his various business activities, he is one of the smartest people I know, a qualified attorney, a true maverick, pragmatic, and a great visionary. He has an uncanny eye for opportunities and the ability to maximize profit from every deal.

Fred initially served in the Dutch army and retired

after a mission in Lebanon where he survived enemy fire which wounded his hand, leading to the loss of an index finger. According to Fred, those few life threatening minutes shaped him for the rest of his career, making him fearless!

I first met Fred over 25 years ago when he was a law enforcement officer in his native Holland working at the Law Enforcement Prosecutors office in The Hague. He was soon elevated to Head officer charged with investigating the distribution of Escobar's (the infamous drug lord) drug dealings into Europe. While working as an active investigating officer, Fred was also building his MLM business on a part-time basis, and studying for an MBA at the same time.

Whenever I visited Holland and Belgium in those days, in the early nineties, to provide training to the troops on behalf of NSA/Juice Plus, I would bump into Fred and we would spend some time together and have great talks. From those humble beginnings, Fred has gone on to become something of a super star in the industry of direct marketing.

After building his MLM organisation on a part-time basis for about 4 years with varying degrees of small successes, he quit the public office and relocated to America. He established himself in Florida and joined a new MLM company and successfully built an organisation in excess of 150,000 people achieving the top pin (rank) level within three years.

After achieving staggering success with his MLM endeavour, he went on to found MADISON TOUCHE LLC, an IT development house specialising in developing compensation architecture and software implementation. Madison Touche became a runaway success and was acquired by Deutsche Bank.

Brimming with much confidence and experiential knowledge from his numerous multi-million dollar successful ventures, Fred ventured into the world of management consulting, marketing his vast experiences to MLM companies looking to launch into the European markets.

He was able to assist the various companies with a full-cycle expertise, from building IT infrastructures, web development, compliance, product development, positioning and marketing, including partnering with the likes of Dr. Oz (Harpo network Oprah's company), and Hank Verkerk.

A lot of the companies Fred consulted for grossed billions in USD sales. Through his consulting platform, Fred had an opportunity to become the license holder for VEMMA Nutrition Company for Europe, Nigeria, Kenya, South Africa, and Israel. As Co-owner and CEO, he was able to take Vemma from a zero starting position to in excess of 200 million euros turnover within 6 years.

After separating from Vemma in 2011, he decided to launch ORIGIN & COMPANY LLC, an MLM entity. Fred was solely responsible for developing the successful lines of nutrition and luxury skincare products, import/export, compliance, product formulation, logistics, IT, marketing and branding, including developing multi-lingual customer support centres. ORIGIN later became his consulting firm to the billion dollar companies he worked with as he developed a reputation as the 'Go To' guy for international expansion.

Fred also founded separately ORIGIN|Unite, a for-profit entity in partnership with AmeriCares, supplying micronutrient treatments for children suffering from malnutrition. It was a program well ahead of its time and, unfortunately, had to cease trading after 4 years when the company ran out of money. He had to sell part of the company to a multi-billion dollar company. Over 50,000 children were taken under the wings or AmeriCares and ORIGIN|Unite and saved from malnutrition. Fred still claims it's the best business he has ever been fortunate to found!

After the bruising experience with Origin, Fred took time out to reflect and re-strategize on his next move. You can't keep a serial entrepreneur down for long. In 2015, he accepted a role as General Manager for the hugely successful multi-billion dollar MLM giant Jeunesse Global LLC, founded in 2009. Jeunesse Global is an MLM manufacturing and distribution company of nutraceuticals and skincare products. Fred is currently assisting Jeunesse to manage their European expansion as GM of Northern Europe.

Here are some of Fred's Accolades:

- The legendary Brian Tracey said this of him: "Fred Stege is one of the most effective marketers in the direct selling industry"

- Achieved multi-millionaire status from building a solid MLM enterprise

- Author of the best seller, _Awaken Your Soul In Network Marketing_, which sold hundreds of thousands of copies and translated into 5 languages.

- Guest lecturer on direct selling case studies at

several Dutch business universities for MBA students and alumni.

- Investor in several wellness ventures.

- Founder of "Aexxis Capital Consortium," a private mutual fund.

Chapter Five:

Crown Yourself as an Emperor or Empress In Your Own Closet

"There is no shortage of remarkable ideas, what is missing is the will to execute them"

- Seth Godin

You have decided on your course of direction. You are sold on your vision and how to execute it. Now, there are three important things that you must be sold on also.

First, you must know your product or service better than anyone else. Second, you must identify and know your customers better than anyone else. Third, you must be driven by a desire so hot that you feel you will burn if you don't give it expression.

Remember, the first expression of the human spirit is desire, which is your spirit craving to give expression to divinity. This means that there is an unquenchable thirst and burden within you to birth what you believe you are carrying within you. This is what many call purpose, and you will keep on trying over and over again to give birth to that purpose. You will never be truly satisfied or fulfilled until you have birthed that purpose.

It does not matter how many times you fail, you will still get the inspiration to get up and dust your pants off, and keep on pursuing the realisation of that purpose. Why? Because it is your raison d'etre. It is the very reason for which you were born, and you will never be truly fulfilled, even with all the money in the world, until you are living your purpose.

This is one of the greatest secrets and mysteries of human achievement, the fact that there is a force inside you that keeps on driving you to be all you were created to be. However, you will need to learn how to keep yourself inspired. I will speak more about this when we come to the chapter on motivation.

For now, my focus is to tell you why I believe you

must crown yourself as an emperor, if you are a man, or an empress, if you are a woman, in your closet. By closet, I mean in private, in obscurity, inside your home, office, or car, where no one can see you, and then make a declaration.

By declaration, I mean several things. First, let us look at what the 19th century Scottish billionaire, Andrew Carnegie, instructed.

"There is a power under your control that is greater than poverty, greater than the lack of education, greater than all your fears and superstitions combined. It is the power to take possession of your own mind and direct it to whatever end you may desire."

That is really powerful! This is what you have to believe before you step out into the world. You must crown yourself as the greatest before anyone tells you. You must believe you can be all you desire to be, and tell yourself that. The late legend, Mohammed Ali, told himself countless times that he was the greatest. His mind believed it and he went out and proved it to the world.

Essentially, you are saying to yourself, "If it is to be, then it is up to me." It is said that man has two creators, his God and himself. Why? Because after you are born, you have to keep recreating yourself almost every day to go in the direction of your most dominant thoughts and desires.

Now, privately begin to speak to yourself and affirm that you are going to make it, and you are going to give the world the beauty of your dream. Everybody can tell you that you won't amount to much in life. This could be your parents, your teachers, your coach, or anybody else for that matter.

You can still defy their predictions and become a roaring success. I am sure you have heard or read stories of many super stars whether in sports, entertainment, or even in the professions, of people who defied all the odds and shocked the world.

The famous motivational speaker, Les Brown, was labelled as uneducable and mentally retarded by his teachers. Today he is the biggest motivational speaker in the world with over $60 million dollars in earnings to date. Do you know why that is? Because it does not matter what the world tells you as long as you don't believe them.

The only thing that can stop you in life is when you accept something to be true! So anybody can say whatever they want about you, as long as you don't believe it. The moment you believe people's prediction or indictment of you, you are done for!

Why is that? Because a man has two creators, his God and himself, that is why. You are the only one with the full authority to accept or reject whatever anybody says about you, and whatever you say about yourself. So the minute you tell yourself something cannot be, then be rest assured that it is not going to be, because you are the only one with the godlike power to create or fashion your own world.

I have told you all this to make this point: crown yourself and anoint yourself as a king or emperor, or as queen or empress, and tell yourself you are going to make it. Then launch out.

Quit waiting for people to approve you or endorse

you, and start approving yourself. If people don't encourage you or make you feel special, then encourage yourself. Declare to yourself that you are a masterpiece, created to perform wonders in the world.

When you tell yourself this repeatedly, you are inadvertently programming your mind for success, through what is known as autosuggestion. This is one of the primary mediums for influencing your subconscious mind.

When you do this, several things happen. First, you are not giving yourself any room for failure. Second, you are stepping out fully persuaded in faith that you are going to succeed. Third, you are instructing your subconscious mind with positive and powerful vibrations of what to believe and what to focus on. Finally, circumstances and situations that align with your dominant thoughts and aspirations will begin to be attracted into your reality.

When you are in motion and moving towards your dream, every obstacle possible will be thrown on your path to dissuade you from succeeding. This is normal and should not come as a surprise to you. The minute you have affirmed to the universe that you are going to make it, the universe in turn tests you to see how committed you are to your own vision, essentially to find out if you believe what you have just declared or affirmed.

It is one thing to say I am going to take over the world, but another thing to have the resilience and determination to bring it to pass. So at this point, you have to focus on strengthening your achievement muscles, just as a weight lifter gently trains up his muscles for strength gradually in other to lift heavier weights.

The other point I want to raise here is this: some of the most successful entrepreneurs do not go out to simply pursue money. They instead fall in love with their product or service and dream of how to bring the service or product to the world to serve or add value to humanity. Usually in the pursuit of this and looking to make a difference with their whole heart, they usually find money being attracted to them in the process.

I guess the point I am making here is this, do not focus on only making money as your overriding pre-occupation. Even though a business exists to make a profit, instead make the delivery of your best effort in terms of products or service as your dominant focus, and in turn it will attract the monetary gains.

When you crown yourself or anoint yourself in obscurity to win, no matter the challenges life throws at you, you will only be thinking of succeeding and not failure. Some of the greatest names out there had to go through tremendous rejections and failures before they triumphed! These are extremely courageous and persistent souls who have usually thrown everything they have into making their ventures successful.

Take for example the owner of the mega-successful Starbucks, Howard Shultz, who heard all the following from potential investors while trying to raise the $1.25 million seed money to launch his first coffee stores, ll Gionale, before he would go on to purchase the world famous Starbucks business. He was told "Americans will never spend a dollar and a half for a cup of coffee," "You are out of your mind," "You should just get a real job."

He was told all of this when he was trying to raise money for his business in 1986. He spoke to 242 investors in the course of a year and 217 said NO! Even though the numerous rejections were heart breaking, his passion, enthusiasm, belief in his dream, and his persistence saw him through and paid off magnificently. Today, his net worth is at $3 billion USD in 2017 according to Forbes.

Today, if you ask anybody what the number one vacuum cleaner is, you will definitely hear the name Dyson at the top of the list. It has replaced the popular Hoover that dominated this market for decades. But, this was not always the case. Sir James Dyson spent 12 years iterating approximately 5,126 trials and errors before the breakthrough came.

The Dyson brand of vacuums without question costs more than any other brand, but they are greatly loved by customers because of their efficiency, unique styling, and simplicity of use. The Dyson product is a great example of a Synthetic vision. Sir James took an everyday household appliance and reinvented it to glowing acclaim.

At this point, as you may have guessed, things did not go swimmingly well from the start for him. In his autobiography 'Against the Odds', Sir James Dyson, who was well acquainted with failing, explained the immense difficulties he encountered during the process of trying to birth his dream. In 2005, he shut down his line of 'contra rotating' washing machines only sold in Britain, because they were haemorrhaging money and too pricey for what the market was prepared to pay.

In Dyson's interview with Bloomberg in 2012, he told them that they spend $2.5 million a week on R&D, and a lot of it was failure. However, he also said what many successful entrepreneurs understand and attest to is that you learn a lot from failure. He continued; "When something is successful, the results are clear to see. Failure however is an enigma. You worry about it, and it teaches you something."

Sir James succeeded because of his dogged determination to succeed even though it nearly bankrupted him. He recounts in his book how he was told, "But James, if there were a better type of vacuum cleaner, Hoover or Electrolux would have invented it."

Sir James consistently attests to the power of dogged determination as the most important trait of an inventor. He said "I have always found that the very moment you are ready to give up, that if you go on a little longer, you end up finding what you are looking for. It is one of life's rewards for perseverance"

Sir James is now one of the world's wealthiest entrepreneurs worth an estimated $4.2 billion and employing over 7000 people worldwide.

Many people would have heard of the name Ursula Burns, one of the most powerful women in the world, according to Forbes in 2009. Ursula literally went from rags to riches. She discovered early that she had a talent for numbers and was really brilliant at it. She rejected the advice from her teachers to pursue a career in nursing or teaching. She had bigger dreams and wanted to do greater things, according to her. The only reason that Ursula could reject the advice from her teachers, was because she had crowned herself as an empress in her closet and was not prepared to settle for less or fall into the usual stereotypes.

Ursula has been chairwoman of Xerox since 2010, and before that she was CEO from 2009 to 2016. She was also the first African-American woman to head a Fortune 500 company.

These are some of the reasons why it is important you first crown yourself as an emperor or empress privately in your closet before you go into the world to sell your idea, product, or service, because if you are not persuaded yourself and determined against all odds to stand by your dream, you will be eaten up by the aggressive wolves and lions in the market place. Your dream will be terminated.

Here is a story of an outstanding lady who would not allow anything to stop her from achieving her dreams. Once Udo had set her mind on the direction of her dreams, and privately crowned herself an empress in her closet, she became unstoppable.

UDO MARYANNE OKONJO'S POTTED STORY

Udo is a truly remarkable and highly accomplished lady in her late-forties. She is a potent mixture of brains, beauty, and class in that order. Udo is hugely successful, both mentally and materially. She is dynamic, confident, and super positive with an engaging winner's personality.

I got to know Udo much better when she engaged my services to host Dr. Emmanuel Kachikwu's launching of 3 great books in Abuja in the autumn of 2016. The event was attended by many dignitaries, including the Vice President of Nigeria, who was chairman of the occasion. Dr. Emmanuel Kachikwu is Nigeria's minister of petroleum, himself a remarkable man, highly accomplished with a towering intellect.

Udo graduated as the best female law student in her year at the Nigerian Law School. She successfully attracted the prestigious British Chevening Scholarship to study law at the University of London, Kings College School of Law where she graduated with a Master's degree in Law (LLM).

The famous Chevening Scholarships are awarded to students who possess leadership qualities from 144 countries around the world, for postgraduate studies in UK universities, and is funded by the British Foreign and Commonwealth Office.

This powerful lady is an alumna of the University of Nigeria, Nsukka, Lagos Business School. Said Business School, University of Oxford. She is also a recent alumna of Cambridge Judge Business School, University of Cambridge, which she attended with the sole purpose of increasing her knowledge of branding and strategy for business growth. Udo personifies clearly the principle of crowning oneself in their closet as an emperor or empress before launching into the market of uncharted waters with their gifts and abilities.

Udo's entrepreneurial awakening began when she was handed a photocopied version of Real Estate guru Robert Allen's classic book, Nothing Down, over 15 years ago while practicing as a corporate and commercial lawyer. Nothing Down literally transformed her life as it gave her a sincere hunger to become a property investor.

She promptly read Allen's second book, Creating Wealth, from real estate, and her search began in earnest. She worked up a huge desire and real fascination with the real estate business, and every Sunday she would drive to various locations around Lagos researching and viewing properties while trying to understand the market.

She did this for about 6 months while still practicing law full time. She would also look through newspapers searching for property listings, prices and movements of the market. She learnt all she could in the locations she was interested in, building up her knowledge and confidence.

Udo became a real estate investor and, spurred by her desire to utilise real estate as a wealth creation vehicle, attended several industry specific courses to sharpen up her knowledge and competency. She qualified for certification from the South African Estate Agency Affairs Board in 2005. She further obtained a certificate in Effective Real Estate Marketing from the National University of Singapore, in conjunction with the Dubai Real Estate Institute in May 2008, amongst several real estate and executive courses.

Then, in 2007, Udo and some partners successfully negotiated and acquired the Fine & Country West Africa license, having realised the immense opportunities that an international Real Estate network could provide. They launched successfully in 2008.

The Fine & Country brand is recognised globally for its unique and versatile blend of smart, strategic and creative marketing, and their professional approach to the sales and leasing of premium residential and commercial properties. Operating out of over 300 locations worldwide, Fine & Country has its head office located on Park Lane, Mayfair, UK. The West African operations are run from Sandton, South Africa, Lagos, Nigeria and Accra, Ghana.

Under Udo's astute and dynamic leadership, the Nigerian operation has leaped to the top in the provision of excellent real estate services to leading real estate developers and institutional clients. Through her visionary and results-orientated leadership, along with her focus and dedication to the growth and development of the Real Estate Industry in Nigeria, Udo was awarded "The Most Influential Personality in Real Estate Award 2014" at the 3rd ADM International Conference on Development. She also received the Awards of Excellence in Accra Ghana, and Real Estate Business Amazon 2014, along with the "BID Europe Award for Excellence 2014", and she was also personally awarded the "ELOY awards 2012" along with the "Mode Man, Woman of the Year Award".

Udo's leadership team for Fine & Country West Africa also received an award in the Gold Category for "Quality, Excellence and Customers Satisfaction" at the 2014 – International Arch of Europe Awards in Frankfurt, Germany.

Today, Udo reigns large as a big mover and shaker in the dynamic industry of real estate, where she and her company are fast becoming the go-to for multinationals, listed corporates, privately held companies, and high net-worth clients. She is very passionate about real estate as a means of wealth creation and nation building.

She also has a huge and relentless passion for leadership development across all sectors of the Nigerian economy and was instrumental in setting up Nigeria's premier 'Real Estate Leaders Network' and the 'Institute of Real Estate Excellence,' amongst other non-real estate related learning platforms.

This amazing and unstoppable lady is the Executive Chairman of Fine & Country West Africa, leading a management team that includes the Country Managing Director from the UK and a Director of Sales / Operations.

Besides her passion for brick and mortar, she is also very passionate about developing people, with several initiatives under her belt, mostly focusing on leadership and personal development. Here are some of her initiatives:

• "Ignite The Champion Within" & "Ignite The Tycoon Within" are platforms she set up for national transformation through empowering and equipping professionals and emerging entrepreneurs to help change mind-sets and unleash the power within.

• Udo is also the founder of the 'iWoW' group (Inspired Women of Worth), a network of women from all over the world which she founded in Johannesburg in 2010. The vision is to inspire, develop, encourage, and promote strong women to fulfil their life's purpose and impact society one family at a time.

• Besides Udo's active involvement in her church, 'This Present House,' she also dedicates her spare time mentoring over 100,000 professionals and entrepreneurs in business and life success through her online platforms.

Udo is a happily married woman and devoted mother of four. She and her husband have recently launched a multi-million-dollar healthy beverage line, set to revolutionise the Nigerian beverage industry.

Chapter Six:

Your Attitude Will Make Or Break You

"Attitude is everything. Life is 10% what happens to you, and 90% how you react to it"

— *Charles R. Swindoll*

Someone once said, and I quote, "a bad attitude is like a flat tire; if you don't change it, you can't go anywhere." How true that statement really is. I once heard a humorous story that demonstrated the power of a positive attitude by always choosing to see "good" in everything.

Once upon a time in Africa, there lived a chief who had a friend with a habit of always seeing something good in every situation. Whatever situation they found themselves in, the friend would always say "this is good!"

One day, the friend went hunting with the chief and helped the chief load his gun, but made an error. When the chief fired the gun, the bullet accidentally shot off his thumb. Dismayed, the chief couldn't believe his eyes and was very angry. His friend, however, made his usual comment by saying yet again "this is good."

The chief angrily retorted, "What can be good about this?" and proceeded to throw his friend in jail. Many months later, the chief was out hunting. This time, he unknowingly found himself in a dangerous part of the jungle where cannibals operated. He was captured by the cannibals, tied up, and prepared to be roasted on the makeshift grill, when suddenly the cannibals discovered he had a thumb missing.

The cannibals conferred among themselves, being very superstitious about the missing thumb of the chief. Since they only ate whole bodied humans without blemish, they decided it might be bad luck to eat the chief and so they set him free.

The chief couldn't believe his luck and ran all the

way to the jail cell where his friend had languished for the last year, and began to profusely apologise to his friend for locking him up all this time. He then told his friend what happened to him and how the missing thumb actually saved his life. He told his friend that he was right, and that it was indeed "good" as his friend said originally.

He asked his friend to forgive him, but his friend told him that it was indeed "good" that he was locked up. The chief said to him surprised "How can it be good to have been locked up all this time?" The friend said to the chief, "Because, if I hadn't been locked up, I would have definitely been with you when you were caught!!"

The morale of the story is to maintain an attitude of positivity, to always look for the good in every circumstance, and things will always turn out for the best!

Whatever line of business or work you are in; you are going to require a great attitude. You cannot escape this reality. When observing successful people like the late Nelson Mandela, Oprah Winfrey, or Richard Branson, one of the first things you notice is their incredibly infectious attitude toward people, success, and life.

For example, there are few businessmen who have been as flamboyant and successful as Richard Branson. The founder of the Virgin Atlantic Airways has unorthodox methods when it comes to doing business, but they work. And chances are that no one has had as much fun on the road to becoming a billionaire than Branson.

He has an uncanny ability to convince anyone of his ambitions and ideals. His desire to push the boundaries of common business practices has made him take on industry giants like British Airways with much success.

And who in Oprah Winfrey's home town of Kosciusko, Mississippi, would have had any idea that she would become the first African American female billionaire and be named as one of the most influential figures of the 20th century?

Speaking recently about her phenomenal success she said, "My philosophy is that not only are you responsible for your life, but doing the best at this moment puts you in the best place for the next moment."

Did you read that? Please read it again and absorb this powerful truth, "doing the best at this moment, wherever you are and in whatever you are doing, positions you for the best in the next moment or opportunity."

I paraphrase slightly!

In other words, these people have what business and life coaches and personal development trainers call a winning attitude, a way of thinking that gives a person total confidence that they will achieve their goals in life.

KAY'S STORY

One such person is my friend Camini Corriette, affectionately known as Kay by her army of friends and customers. Besides her tenacity, one of the major keys to Kay's success has been her attitude towards people and life. Kay was sent to the UK from Guyana by her parents at the age of seventeen to study. With scarcely any relatives in the UK, she had to rely on herself. Fortunately, she had very good grounding from back home and determined to be a success in the UK.

When things became extremely difficult and she could have easily returned back home to mummy and daddy in Guyana, she decided against it. She didn't want to disappoint her parents, who had spent a lot of money bringing her and keeping her there.

Her motivation was first, respect for family and second, respect for herself. That was her chief driving force. Kay married young and had her daughter, Nicole, but soon found marriage was not what she wanted. In her own words she said, "I realized that I made a mistake".

She was married to an older and wiser man. She didn't want to blame her husband for her mistake, but there were things she wanted to experience in life which she couldn't with her marriage. One of her primary goals was to raise Nicole successfully and to maintain as high a quality standard of living in the UK as she had back home.

So the bars she set for herself were very high, and when she left her husband, he told her that she could go and queue for the 'Dole,' a government Social Security handout for unemployed people. She said to herself, "I'll show him!" despite the obstacles he put in her way!

When she came to the UK, she trained as a hair dresser in European hair working for a European saloon. She also trained on black hair when she worked for a black owned saloon during her short stay in Spain. It was there that she noted how the black saloon owners had more money than sense. She observed all the mistakes they made and determined not to make similar mistakes.

When her marriage failed, she took up a part-time job working in hair saloons while she was plotting how to start her own business. She had always dreamed of owning her own business, but she did not know how to raise the finance to do so. She approached the banks and they turned her down repeatedly.

When she asked them to use her home as collateral, the banks told her "No, Mrs. Corriette. We are not in the habit of taking people's homes away from them," already assuming she was going to fail! But since she believed so much in her dream of opening her own hairdressing saloon, she pressed on and eventually approached a broker who was able to help her raise the £12,000 she required back in 1985 to open her business.

Even though she had a measure of fear and wasn't sure how she was going to repay the money, the pull of her dream was stronger and she went for it. She hasn't looked back since. At the time she opened her saloon, there weren't many black saloons around and she literally built her business by one person at a time through the power of word of mouth.

She gave people the type of service they craved, a truly personal and friendly service. This helped her build a solid client base, with many of these people becoming great friends, and developing a wonderful community spirit with everyone.

I personally have known Kay for over twenty-five years, and have been a witness to her many trials and successes. More importantly, I have seen how her positive spirit and wonderful attitude towards life has won her many fans.

Besides her attitude toward her friends and clients is her attitude toward her bank. Even though they didn't offer her the money initially to start her business, she has become good friends with her bank manager over the years. She normally pops in every year with gifts for her manager, and he in turn has kept an eye out for her.

Even when she has gone into the red occasionally, the bank always looked out for her. She, in turn, honours the relationship by calling in and letting them know when she can correct the deficit!

When things were difficult in the past, she taxed her mind and came up with other opportunities to bring in some cash. By leveraging her skills and experience, she was able to teach hairdressing during her quiet periods.

Kay's business and her daughter also kept her grounded and disciplined over the years. She has become a more stable and wiser individual, both in her business and personal life. Because of the pressures associated with running her business, she has learnt to conduct breathing exercises to manage stress.

She recons things go wrong in your life. When you are all tense and unhappy, because of all the negative energy, you have to find calm in your life. Only you can develop that. Nobody can do it for you. Kay is a svelte and trim sixty something year old. She looks the picture of brimming health and vitality, and she is having the time of her life.

Her daughter, Nicole, is very settled as a practicing physician in a London hospital. Kay also began quietly accumulating a property portfolio before it became fashionable in England. Her property portfolio now consists of 5, including her saloon, and her apartment in Marbella in Spain. She drives her beloved Mercedes SLK, and she says life is good.

When I caught up with her recently, she was just putting the finishing touches to her latest venture. She told me this was going to be her retirement business. Her new venture is promoting African and Caribbean artists in Fine Art; she wants to create more understanding between Africa and the Caribbean, a kind of a bridge between the two continents.

She wants to teach diversity while promoting Fine Art, and plans to have like-minded groups of people go away on artistic holidays to countries in Africa, Spain, France, Italy and the Caribbean, where they learn to paint and exercise. She sees herself going into her retirement years doing her lifestyle business, doing something she loves.

WHAT IS A WINNING ATTITUDE?

A winning attitude is, quite simply, a positive way of thinking and behaving towards somebody or something. Attitude is what helps you to set the stage for high achievement. Whether you are, for example, trying to launch your business, improve your relationships, or buy a house you've always dreamed of, there is a saying that you are only an attitude away from success.

Your attitude is what enables you to positively or negatively interpret situations, which then dictates your response to it. Also, you will observe that wherever you see somebody doing an excellent job, you can be sure that person has a winning attitude. A positive attitude is infectious, and most successful entrepreneurs and achievers have attitudes worth catching.

In his powerful book and runaway best seller, _The Purpose Driven Life_, author Rick Warren said "Your thinking determines your feelings, and your feelings influences your actions, so your attitude in life is dictated by the way you think, which means we have a choice in the matter."

We have a choice in deciding what type of attitudes we want to exhibit. So, for example, if you think you are poor, then that is an attitude of your mind! And as the legendary Dr Norman Vincent Peale said in his book, _The Power of a Positive Mental Attitude_, "Believe you are defeated, believe it long enough, and it is likely to become a fact."

A winning attitude is critical because the journey to the top is usually fraught with challenges, competition, adaptation, and hard work. To climb the success ladder, you will probably have to deal with prejudice, rejection or discrimination, whether of age, race, gender, or class. The right kind of attitude will help you overcome all of these obstacles.

The good news is that everyone can develop great attitudes, and so can you!

Dr William James, who is recognized as the father of American psychology, said, "Your attitude in life will always determine your altitude." The better your attitude, the higher you will soar.

For example, the potential business owner or someone already in business should ask themselves these important questions: "What kind of attitude do I bring to service? Am I doing all I can to provide my clients with the best possible service? Am I aiming to provide professionalism, courtesy, and excellence? These are critical questions for the person in business to ask.

You see, winning attitudes can also be developed in other areas of life besides the workplace. Let's take the person who wants to be a great parent. Do you inspire your children with confidence and a 'can do' attitude? Is the way you live congruent with your teachings to your children? Do you, for example, tell them not to use bad language and then they hear you swearing regularly? Or do you tell them, for example, that everyone is equal and then they hear you use less than flattering, discriminatory language because of somebody's ethnicity or tribe?

And what is your attitude towards friends and colleagues who are more successful in their professional or personal lives? Are you excited for them? Do you encourage them or are you envious, jealous, or resentful and tear them down? Whether or not someone seems more successful than you, you can still develop and adopt a winning attitude. And what you radiate you will always attract.

Here are some thoughts on attitude for you to Meditate on:

"Aerodynamically, the bumble bee shouldn't be able to fly; but it doesn't know it, so it continues to fly." – Mary Kay Ash

My thoughts: Always practice possibility thinking. Focus on possibilities, not impossibilities.

"A pessimist is a person who, regardless of the present, is disappointed in the future"- Anonymous

My thoughts: Always practice positive thinking. It is superior to negative thinking.

"We do not see things as they are, we see things as we are" – Herb Cohen

My thoughts: Constantly work on improving your self-image.

"Where you are today is the sum total of your thoughts; you will be tomorrow where your thoughts take you." -James Allen

My thoughts: Maintain a positive mental attitude and commit to seeing yourself at your best.

"Life's battles do not always go to the stronger or faster man, but sooner or later, the man who wins is the man who thinks he can". – Bruce Lee

My thoughts: Never, ever give up; believe you will achieve your dreams eventually.

"When one door shuts, another opens; but we often look so regretfully at the closed door that we do not see the new one that has opened for us" -Alexander Graham Bell

My thoughts: Maintain an attitude of expectancy, expect to win.

"Circumstances do not make the man. They reveal the man to himself" -James Allen.

"Before a person can achieve the kind of life he wants, he must think, act, walk, talk and conduct himself in all of his affairs as would the person he wishes to become" - Zig Ziglar

My thoughts: Before you can become it, you must first think it, act it, and believe it in your mind.

HOW TO CULTIVATE A WINNING ATTITUDE

One of the most vital steps you can take toward achieving your greatest potential in your business is to learn to monitor and manage your attitude towards your work, employees, and professional relationships.

You have to work towards disciplining your inner conversations with yourself. Stop and ask yourself, whenever your mind begins to wonder off towards the negative, "Is this thought positive and empowering to me, or is it negative, disempowering, and destructive?"

Decide to choose a dialogue that motivates you and reject thoughts of self-pity. You can do it! You have the power, you only need to decide.

Stuff happens, and as long as we are 6 feet above the ground (alive), stuff is going to happen. Top entrepreneurs are people who have learnt to live and thrive in uncertainties.

As stuff happens, decide how you are going to respond. Use power words like, this is great, amazing, wonderful, excellent, wow. Then go about finding what is wonderful, amazing, great, or wonderful about the situation.

You will be surprised at how, just by maintaining a

positive mind-set and using positive words, you psychologically send power messages to your subconscious, and train it to get in the habit of managing tough and initially disappointing news.

That is so much better than using self-defeating and disempowering words like, "Oh no. I am finished. I am dead. We are done for. What are we going to do?" and so forth. It is the messages, and feelings, you send to your subconscious mind that it feeds on, and that it will in turn feed back to you in whatever situation you find yourself.

Train your mind and mouth never to speak words of fear or panic. This will take a little time to master if you are not already in the practice of doing this. Entrepreneurship will throw so many challenges and some real problems at you. You must train yourself to deal with it all.

Here are 10 key steps to developing great attitude:

• Make a decision that you will become a person of great attitude, that is the first step.

• Make a habit of practicing positive thinking by training your mind to think positive day-by-day.

• Learn to mirror people with great attitudes, because most successful entrepreneurs have great attitudes and they radiate cool, calm and relaxed confidence. Watch how they look, walk, talk and act.

• Train your mind to focus on the best of life, rather than the worst from life.

• Practice treating everyone you come in contact with, small or great, as if they were the most important person on earth.

- Smile. Always use this universal language of acceptance when you come in contact with anyone, whether it is your staff, customers, or other relationships.

- Understand the fact that people will give their money, their love, and their respect to you if you make them feel appreciated.

- Entrepreneurs and business owners always look to make profit, and there is nothing wrong with that. However, it must be profit at the service of people, and not at the expense of people. By all means make a handsome profit, but profit only after delivering your best service and value!

- Spend 80% of your time developing your attitude and 20% focused on skill development.

- Everyday ask this power question to yourself: how can I increase my service today? Why? Because greater rewards will come from your improved service.

Do you know that your attitude speaks? Yes, it has a voice, and you can always tell somebody's attitude by just observing them, from their welcome and positive smiles, to their positive "all things are possible" way of speaking.

Remember, it is our attitude towards life that determines life's attitude toward us as the legendary Earl Nightingale taught. And it is our attitude toward others that will determine their attitude toward us!

Look, life is searching for people who believe they

are in charge here on earth, people who expect the universe to give way to them when they show up! When you meet these people you can always tell, whether they are serving you in the bank, at a restaurant, airport, or across the table in a business negotiations meeting. You cannot miss a person of positive attitude, because it cannot be hidden.

Begin to act like you know where you are going and the world will move out of your way! So commit to having the best attitude. Begin today and practice speaking about only the best things you want to happen for the next 30 days. You will be astonished by the results you will get with regards to problems, family, business, colleagues, and people.

And as Mahatma Gandhi said, *"Let us become first the change we wish to see in the world."*

Here's to your great attitude!

Chapter Seven:

Understanding Your Differential Advantage

"If you
don't have a
competitive
advantage,
don't compete"
-Jack Welch

The iconic Elon Musk, one of Silicon Valley's most exciting futurists, who is the founder and CEO of SolarCity, SpaceX, and the beautiful Tesla brand of cars said in a recent 2016 interview with CNBC that, *"There is a pretty good chance that we all end up with a universal basic income salary, or something like that, due to automation."*

Is this an impossible or far-fetched idea from the genius Musk?

Not really! An advanced economy like Switzerland actually toyed with the idea of instituting a universal basic monthly salary of 2,500 Swiss francs, approximately $2578, in the summer of 2016, but the great people of Switzerland rejected the offer. Can this be then that the idea is potentially upon us?

Even former President of the United States, Barack Obama, had a similar conversation with MIT's Lab while he was in office. He discussed the idea and possibility of a universal basic income, whether it is the right model, and if it would be popular and accepted by the majority of the populace. What is clear is the world has begun this debate and it will be heating up over the next 10 – 20 years.

Why all this talk about the possibilities of a universal basic salary? Because, as you may have noticed, the world is fast advancing into an age of automation and robotics. Computers, intelligent machines, and robots are looking more likely as the future workforce. More and more jobs will be replaced by technology.

People will become more and more unnecessary as they have less and less work to do. This is why the discussions are now taking place in the advanced economies of how to sustain the livelihoods of the people if or when they potentially get replaced by machines.

According to a January 2017 UK Guardian article, the World Economic Forum is predicting that robotic automation will result in the net loss of more than 5 million jobs across 15 developed nations by 2020. This is a conservative estimate.

Another study, conducted by the International Labour Organization, states that as many as 137 million workers across Cambodia, Indonesia, the Philippines, Thailand, and Vietnam – approximately 56% of the total workforce of those countries – are at risk of displacement by robots, particularly workers in the huge outsourced garment manufacturing industry.

Recently, the prestigious Oxford University researchers have estimated that 47 percent of U.S. jobs could potentially be at risk or could be automated in the next 10 to 20 years. Many workers will have the shock of their lifetime coming to them if they are not prepared.

THE POTENTIAL IMPLICATIONS TO THE JOBS MARKET

The field of robotics can potentially be the most important and, without question, the most disruptive technological shift since the industrial revolution. Experts now believe that we are at a tipping point in an imminent robotic deployment. Most importantly, much of the developed world simply isn't prepared for such a radical transition.

What this tells me is that if you have not found your unique niche and developed your differential advantage, where you have become a specialist or developed your unique expertise in something, then you are potentially in danger of being replaced by a machine sometime soon. Many people will be affected by the invasion of these machines as they begin to do work in supremely less time than humans.

Machines don't take a break. They don't sleep, nor do they require vacations. Some of these machines actually have the ability to repair themselves or build new parts should they become faulty. One of these machines, as an example cited by Martin Ford, author of, Rise of the Robots, is that a Robot can prepare and flip a gourmet hamburger in less than 10 seconds flat.

They could soon replace an entire McDonalds crew. However, the threat is not only to lower – skilled workers, as University trained people, such as professionals like lawyers, pilots, and doctors who do predictable things could also have great competition from Artificial Intelligence.

Just think about it. Machines don't go out drinking at night, or take drugs, or fight with their spouse before coming to work and have to perform a precarious surgery on their patients with unsteady or unclear eyes and minds. Once machines are programmed, they can deliver with electrifying accuracy and precision.

OUR CURRENT AGE

In this Psychozoic age of the mind, or digital and knowledge based age, where competition is rifer than the world has ever seen it, how do you stand out? How do you compete with your product or service? How do you capture a slice of the huge global business?

To be in a position to really compete, you must identify and develop your differential advantage, or what advertisers and sales people call your unique selling perspective (USP) or competitive edge. I call it the seat of your power!

The truth is, in order to succeed or survive in our hugely competitive world, you must possess specialized knowledge in something. What will make people choose to do business with you, or buy your product or service, instead of your competitors? So the key question really is what aspect or combination of aspects will separate you or your business from the others?

Now, you have to think about this carefully. Are you going to compete by delivering superior service? Will it be a wider range of products selection or a customized service? Will it be more favourable with longer opening hours for example? Or will you be offering easier payment terms?

And in terms of the marketing and sales industry, are you a tried and tested leader? Do you have a strong reputation as someone who helps others get results so you can mentor people to quick success? Do you have a solid and trusted reputation for integrity, or a combination of some of these?

A differential advantage essentially makes you a better choice or option against your competitors in the mind of your prospects, clients, or customers. You must remember that perception - what a person believes -is reality to them. And what we believe tends to influence the actions we take more than what is actually true.

To truly succeed in today's volatile world, we must find ways of distinguishing ourselves in the market place. We have to keep reminding ourselves that we are all in sales, whether we are selling plastic surgery, real estate, investments, insurance, nutrition or political office.

So the key question to ponder here is, how easy is it to find somebody else to do what you do or replace your product or service? Those who are going to succeed and stand out will be those who know precisely where they fit in the market place. The focus right now must be on how to boost your value, wherever you are.

If you, through your products or services, can help organisations or individuals reduce cost pressures or help them become more competitive and profitable, then they want to work with you. People are usually prepared to give you a try if you can help solve their problems. Your focus must be repeatedly asking how you can increase your maximum value and execute with precision to distinguish yourself from your competition.

The power of your branding is essentially the art of influencing the perceptions of people, to make them believe you are of benefit to them.

ELLIOTT'S STORY

Finally, here is the story of my good friend and former business partner, Elliott Omose. Elliott and I were involved in a start-up company a few years ago. I was vice president of the African markets for Origin corporation, a dynamic start-up with a huge dream of combating malnutrition among children at-risk populations utilising potent nutritional products. Elliot was appointed as our Nigeria country director and we worked closely together and became very good friends.

Elliott's story is one of a man with huge vision and who understood the high importance of competing with his differential advantage in a dynamic and aggressive market.

Elliott made the decision to launch a couple of entrepreneurial initiatives 3 years ago in Nigeria. He had harboured these ideas for a little while and sensed it was time to make the move into a volatile and aggressive market with only his dream and determination to succeed against all the odds stacked against him.

As Elliott informed me, he had wasted nearly 50 years of his life before discovering the greatest law that governs the stewardship and control of large wealth. He discovered very late, but not too late, in life that most of the elite class that control large wealth pursue something far bigger than wealth itself. The wealth is the effect!

His dream began nearly ten years ago when he stumbled on a World Health Organisation (W.H.O) article that stated diabetes will be a bigger challenge to the economy of Nigeria than even corruption and poor infrastructure in the coming decades. Prior to reading the article, he had harboured the dream of penetrating Nigeria as a major business target, not necessarily because he is originally Nigerian; but as a trained and intrepid entrepreneur he knew he could not afford to miss a dynamic market of over 186 million consumers, a massive population when compared to the UK where he lived.

Elliott believes that true greatness, success, or wealth, is but a reward for great value contributed. He made up his mind to only contribute rare and impactful values. He advises people not to go for what everyone else is offering, but to instead make the decision to become a premium value contributor to society and wealth will be attracted to you in rapid rate. He made a decision never to attach his name to anything common, but instead to focus on high premium products.

Elliott is a great student of the Bible. He uses the example of Zacchaeus, the tax collector who wanted to meet Jesus but realised he was too short to be noticed in the crowd. So what did he do? He ran ahead and took a conspicuous position on a tree. Jesus and the crowd eventually noticed him as they were passing by and he soon became an overnight sensation.

When Elliott realised he didn't have all the required resources to launch out, he decided, like Zacchaeus, to run ahead and position himself quickly. That is what he did and, as they say, the rest is history.

Elliott came up with a concept that would introduce him, as opposed to him introducing the concept. He made up his mind to write himself into the future pages of Nigeria. He decided that when the story of diabetes and the fight against diabetes in Nigeria is told, it won't be complete without his contribution.

Elliott hired a team of researchers who discovered and reported back to him that his first attention must be focused on the Nigerian diet culture. He decided to introduce a healthier version of popular, common, and traditional dishes like pounded yam, eba, semo and fufu, all strongly rooted in high levels of starch.

These dishes accompany traditional soups in the various regions of the country. Elliott launched "Elkris Super-Oat" with beta glucan, clinically proven to reduce cholesterol and a healthier alternative to high carbohydrates.

However, the launch of Elkris almost failed as no shop or retailer was interested. Those that had the shelf space told him to dump the products in their shop and wait to see if anyone requested them. Most advised him to go and spend a fortune on TV and radio advertising and promotion, and when the public becomes familiar with the brand, he could come back to them.

The other major issue was the business model he created, asking for his money up-front before delivering goods. Everyone told him he must be crazy or dreaming; that even Dangote the richest man in the country distributed products on a sell and return money basis. They asked him who he thought he was with an unknown product, requesting this?

Fortunately, he had a few options to fall back on to prevent the early death of the brand before it saw daylight. His years of successful MLM experience in the UK were to become an invaluable asset to him. He had benefitted from over 5 years of top training on guerrilla marketing, where he learned concepts to generate critical exposure at the fastest possible time without the costly TV or radio advertising.

So using unconventional approaches, he tried referral MLM as a vehicle to first break the ground and introduce the brand before launching it as a main stream product. In less than two years, from a product that nearly failed, it is now in every major supermarket, shop, and retail outlet in Nigeria. And, incidentally, he still gets upfront payment before supplying which is extremely rare in Nigeria and a testament to the quality and high demand of the Elkris brand of Super-Oat.

Also, in less than 2 years, Elkris products have received highly coveted national and African awards for innovation. His product received the "Diabetes friendly/management food of the year" for 2016. Secondly, a personal leadership award was presented to Elliott a couple of months ago from "The Kwame Nkrumah Foundation" in recognition of his contribution to the health of Africa. It is a rare award reserved for dignitaries and captains of industry in Africa.

In its first 6 months of preliminary operations, they already have the likes of state and federal ministries of health, World Health Organisation, and World Bank looking at how to partner with his company's CSR (Stop-Diabetes Foundation) and looking at how to support their Diabetes Awareness Campaign.

Today, in shops across Nigeria, Elliott comes in contact with people who are introducing his own products to him, not knowing he is the manufacturer. He enjoys listening to people speak to him with passion about his own product. The greatest joy for him is in walking away at the end without introducing himself as the manufacturer.

Here are some success tips from Elliott:

1.   He helpfully advises that should you desire to control large wealth, and/or a great legacy of recognition; leave the money and instead:

2.   See money as a "Reward" which people are prepared to send to you ceaselessly, for the rare value(s) you are contributing in enriching their lives.

3.   Champion a worthy course outside of yourself, and pursue it with passion, alongside your chosen primary rare value(s) of either products or services

With the above in mind, here are the two personal and private crusades that drive Elliott's true passion to generate wealth in the ensuing years.

Elliot's Strategic Intention

1.   Is to light up the dark villages of the interiors of Africa with the good news of Jesus Christ, by erecting 1000 new rural church buildings across the most remote regions of Africa, where villagers have been worshiping under trees. He wants posterity to remember him as the first Christian who is not a pastor or church overseer and single-handedly streamed $100 million from business into erecting 1,000 church buildings throughout the forgotten villages of Africa with NO outside donations.

2.   By 2020, to reach and prevent 1 million pre-diabetic Nigerians from slipping into full-blown diabetes status. Under the platform of Stop-Diabetes Awareness Foundation (Stodaf), I have therefore decided to:

Educate at least 500,000 Nigerians every year on diabetes and its prevention; through

o   Free diabetes check-ups outreach

o   Telephone diabetes consultations

o   Recommend better dietary alternatives

o   Hold talks on diabetes for interest-groups

o   Conduct seminars, and symposiums on diabetes and its prevention

o   Host an annual marathon known as #RunFrom-Diabetes

3. Approaching the art of generating wealth from the perspective of the above two strategic intentions is what has turned me from an average player into an instant giant on the inside. I gave myself 25 years to phase all of these. This has turned me into a destination/time bound, highly-driven locomotive. As a result, I noticed that rare wealth generating concepts come to me easily.

The Elkris Group is currently expanding into the rest of Africa, implementing a service blueprint to be the choice provider for food, fashion, and shelter for 2 million African consumers by 2025.

COMPETING WITH YOUR BRAND AS PART OF YOUR DIFFERENTIAL ADVANTAGE

In this Digital Age, the correct branding has become extremely important. As a matter of fact, your brand may mostly be the differentiating factor between you and your competitors. This is why businesses and entrepreneurs manage their brands meticulously.

They know that, in the eyes of the customer, perception is reality. What your client or customer perceive in their minds to be true, is reality to them. Your brand, quite simply, is based on you or your company's characteristics and attributes. People will look into this and decide whether they like you and want to do business with you or not.

The Amazon founder Jeff Bezos said that your brand is what other people say about you when you are not in the room. You have to fight to become distinctive in the market or definitely within your chosen niche. If you are trying to appeal to everyone, it can be counterproductive and dilute your appeal.

Once you clearly have an understanding of your target market, then do some work to understand what your target market wants or needs and endeavour to fulfil it. All you are trying to accomplish here is creating your own distinctive identity within a niche.

Take a restaurant like Nandos, the extremely successful fast-food chicken restaurant chain dominant in the UK for the past 17 years. Nandos sells itself as the home of the legendary Portuguese flame grilled peri-peri chicken. Peri-peri simply means pepper sauce in Swahili.

My children love and swear by it. My wife and I equally love their extra hot chicken, and especially their Mediterranean salad with feta cheese. Nandos has been able to attract obsessive levels of loyalty from everyone from superstar celebrities like David Beckham and Beyoncé, to blue blooded royalty like Prince Harry.

Even politicians like former PM David Cameron have been spotted at Nandos, not to mention the army of dedicated teenage followers as their regular favourite chicken joint. So what is the secret of Nandos?

For one, it has a truly classless appeal. You can spot anyone from high middle classes, to the teenager on his first date with his girlfriend, enjoying the food. If you happen to work for some key agencies like the military, NHS, The Ambulance, Police, Fire Service etc. as long as you present your ID, you will automatically be entitled to 20 per cent discount of your order.

Next is the simplicity of their menu choices combined with a truly amazing consistency of taste. Frankly, nobody is interested in dealing with a company that they cannot rely on for consistency. That is one of the greatest put-offs for discerning customers.

I can personally attest to certain restaurants that began well, and a couple of them were actually owned by my friends, but after 3 different occasions when I was dissatisfied with a particular offering, I made a gentle complaint to the manager, and later to the owner, who is my friend.

I took guests to this same restaurant on two different occasions and ordered this particular dish I enjoy very much, but it was still the same, bland and not as tasty. I had enough and took my business somewhere else. Incidentally, it was just down the road from this other restaurant. This other restaurant delivers the dish the way I like it and 2 years later they are still enjoying my patronage.

Some of the characteristics or attributes of your brand people look at either corporately or personally may be some of the following:

- Your Appearance

- Your consistency

- Your cleanliness
- Your Professionalism
- Your leadership
- Your skills
- Your results
- Your reputation
- Your personality
- Your charisma
- Your spirit of excellence
- Your authenticity
- Your reliability
- Your accountability
- Your problem solving abilities
- Your customer services

Chapter Eight:

Selling Yourself And Your Ideas – The Difference Maker

Without sales nothing happens, the whole world stops

-Charles Ajayi-Khiran

The Dragon's Den is a successful TV show in the UK where entrepreneurs, impresarios, and inventors pitch their ideas, concepts or products to a panel of five wealthy investors in exchange for a slice of their business. The thing to remember is that the Dragons are not only looking for a great idea, but they are also observing how the individuals sell themselves as well.

When you watch the program and observe how the entrepreneurs present themselves and pitch their business ideas to the Dragons you then begin to notice the high importance of the ability to sell yourself, concept or product.

Shark Tank is the American television series equivalent, where six very tough self-made millionaires and billionaire tycoons invest in American businesses and products with the opportunity to help the successful entrepreneurs become millionaires. Aspiring entrepreneurs get the opportunity to present their ideas to the Sharks made up of the business tycoons, and try to convince them to invest money in their ideas.

When you watch programmes like these, you see how critically important selling skills are and the ability to sell yourself or your concept or product really is. For those with the skills and ability to sell themselves, you notice they get off to a very quick and convincing start by winning the attention and interest of the potential investors immediately.

Nothing in this world happens without sales because without sales, business cannot happen. Everybody sells, whether a dentist, plastic surgeon, inventors, investment bankers, lawyers, politicians, school teachers, real estate agents, software writers, authors, pastors, imams, Rabbi's, fashion designers, restaura-teurs, wealth managers, etc.

I believe without question that entrepreneurs need to learn this very valuable skill. It is one thing to come up with the greatest idea or concept, it is another thing to be able to articulate it in a convincing and persuasive manner and have the world or investors eating out of your hands or salivating at the thought of your proposition.

Many entrepreneurs don't get this point. They find it difficult to put their thoughts together, with the confidence, boldness, and poise to sell the idea to their target, whoever that may be. Learning sales skills will be invaluable to you for so many reasons which I will list out below.

You see, no matter how superb your product or idea is, if you do not come across as competent, warm, and likeable, you may struggle to attract the right people or investments to your cause.

Just think about how many entrepreneurs have gone to their banks or to business angels with their ideas and business plans. They are quizzed about the viabilities or mechanics of their product. While they wait for the entrepreneur to persuade them or convince them, imagine how many waffle and bore the living daylights out of the investor?

Even with formal education, so many fumble, and stammer their way through the process. So many could not answer questions convincingly nor sell themselves dynamically. These people eventually leave without the commitment or funding they are seeking.

If your business is young and you are just starting out, then this skill becomes critical. You can't escape sales. You must know how to move people if you intend to build a great enterprise, and sales skills will do that for you.

In Daniel Pink's excellent book, To Sell is Human, he explains that we all now spend about 40% of our time trying to move others. To be a great and successful entrepreneur, you must become a great salesperson!

7 POWERFUL THINGS SALES SKILLS WILL DO FOR YOU

1.   Learn and develop rapport building skills. The following tips will help you connect quickly with your client or investor:

-   Wear a suit. If you don't want to wear a tie, that is okay, but wear a suit or smart jacket or blazer, unless you are in the technology business, in which case you may get away with your jeans and T-shirt.

-   Work on your smile. Make it warm, friendly, and natural.

-   Develop a firm handshake, not a 'dead fish kind of limp, no power handshake.' Don't squeeze too hard, just enough for them to feel your energy.

-   Find something true to compliment quickly about them. If you can't find anything you can genuinely compliment, then don't.

-   Look them in the eye when speaking. Don't avoid eye contact or they may wonder if you are hiding something.

- Quickly look for areas where you have common ground, if any. This helps you to connect naturally.

2.   Develop a selling and closing style that suits you and that you are comfortable with. Whether that is:

- Consultative selling. Essentially, consulting with the client and establishing needs before the mention of product or service comes in. The interchanging or the dialogue between you and the client is key, in order to understand before proffering the correct solutions or

- Relationship selling. Your attention is more focused on the interaction between you and the client and building rapport, rather than in the product details or price, or

- Solution selling. This is where you take the time to find out the client's important needs, and you direct them to the appropriate solution, whether product or service.

There are many other selling techniques. Discover which suits your natural style and stick to it.

3.   Develop a strong and irresistible pitch. Write a script of how you want to come across introducing your offering. This is important to help you flow and stay in control. I don't mean like a sales script, but rather like a marketing document introducing yourself and proposition strongly.

Ensure it is one that draws your client or customer in using the right choice of words that settles your client and engages their hearts and minds. Explain why you do what you do and your mission and how it will benefit them. Make the script very brief.

4. Sales skills and training will prepare you to hear the word NO and not take it personally. No is never usually a personal rejection of you, it may just mean the timing isn't right for them, or there may be no immediate need for your product or service, or maybe they can't afford your product or service. It is not a personal rejection. You will get many No's in your entrepreneurial journey, so get comfortable with hearing that word.

5. Practice the art of dynamic listening. Listening hard is one of the toughest things that you do in sales. To be a great listener means that when your client is speaking, you are really engrossed in his or her words. You are not thinking of answers to counteract as they are speaking.

When you listen well, you will be surprised at how many clues the client gives away. Sometimes, they may even tell you all you need to close the deal or know which direction to lead the conversation. Sales is not about just blabbing and non-stop talking. Top professionals are superb listeners, because they know great listening will cut down their work quickly.

6. Learn to close and ask for the deal. It is sad how many entrepreneurs spend all their time talking and never asking for the deal. Many feel so uncomfortable having to close. It should not be so; it should be a natural flow at the end of your conversation or presentation. There are several ways you can ask for the deal, here are some ideas;

-   Having heard the details about the product or service, is this something you are excited about becoming a part of?

- It would really be a privilege to have someone with your immense experience and weight backing us, are you happy for us to proceed?

- How would you like to proceed?

- Is there anything stopping you from moving forward now?

7. Learn to be comfortable with a pause or silence. Sales skills will teach you how to be comfortable with a pregnant pause or silence. Many people are very uncomfortable with silence, as a matter of fact they panic thinking something is wrong. Some of the biggest decisions are made in silence.

As I have mentioned before, I have a billionaire client that I advise, and he is one of the very best when it comes to silence or a prolonged pregnant pause. He is very measured in his response and he does not speak too quickly. He listens well and, even when asked questions, he really takes his time so that you are almost tempted to jump into his head and pull out the answer. But guess what? When he speaks, it is almost usually positive.

After you have asked for the sale, keep your mouth shut. I know this is difficult, but you are going to have to learn to practice this art. Usually we say in sales the first person to speak loses. Just look at the client and wait patiently for what he or she has to say. You will be surprised that it is usually a strong positive response.

Next I want to tell you the story of a young man who used great sales skills powerfully to his advantage. These helped him become a dynamic and successful entrepreneur. I am immensely proud of this young man. I worked with him for over 6 months as his executive coach in London.

I always saw greatness in him, and I did not fail to tell him so many times how big he will become. He is a brilliant salesman, audacious and courageous, the traits and characteristics of dynamic entrepreneurs. This is his story in his own words:

GBITE ODUNEYE'S STORY

Life is a sum of all your choices, it's a reflection of your thought process, and the way one perceives the World. So, we are the architects of our own world. We can achieve and be whatever and whoever we set our minds on being.

As far back as I remember, I have always been curious, and had a thirst and hunger for knowledge. I have always wondered why things are the way they are. This has always been a fundamental trait of mine.

In terms of my potted history, I grew up as the middle child of a brilliant family that always allowed my siblings and I to be individuals and develop an identity for ourselves. For that, I will always remain grateful to my parents. They allowed me to interact with the world to learn and understand how things work.

Like many, I attended a boarding secondary school at the Nigerian Navy and, on completion of my SSCE, I travelled to England to study Economics and Politics in Bristol.

During my time at University, I worked on several

events that sharpened my entrepreneurial skills and gave me a taste of creating value for people.

After graduation, I worked as a trainee broker and started my career in Financial Services. The buzz was electric. I had found my calling and I enjoyed my early days in the sector.

Things changed when my father proposed to the Federal Government of Nigeria the 'Nigerian Heritage Park' in Abuja, capital of Nigeria. It was going to be a Heritage site like no other with Museums, Hotels, Amusement Parks, Libraries etc.

The project got approval after 2 years of lobbying but, unfortunately, our financiers pulled out because of the World Economic crash in 2008. It was terribly distressing as we had invested so much money and time on the project. Importantly, it changed my life and thought processes forever and put me on the path I ride on today.

Based on what we all hear about Africa, what happened was very interesting. My father had just had a stroke and was recovering in London. At the time, he was in his late sixties. During his recovery process, he thought up the Nigerian Heritage Park.

We wrote a proposal together, and I sent it by courier to the then President of Nigeria –Rtd General Obasanjo. Truth be told, I was happy to do it because it would keep my old man busy. Doctors had mentioned to me that activity was good for his recovery.

To my surprise, President Obasanjo responded and invited us to present the project in Abuja. During the 2 years, I met and presented the project to several high profile people I had read about for years. I interacted with all living past presidents of Nigeria because of the project.

Remember, I sent the courier just to make my Dad happy, but see all the positive things that transpired from that action? A gentleman in his late sixties who had just had a stroke, with a keyboard and a little imagination, gave me the best work experience ever.

It awakened the voice of my soul. Since your mentality shapes your reality, it was fair to say my reality from that moment changed forever as I saw the world differently.

From that moment on, I was hell bent on creating my own reality. For me to achieve that, I would need a focussed and persistent mind-set, and would need to seek out partners and mentors that would enable me grow and give me strength when things didn't go my way.

In the years that followed, I learned a lot from both my successes and failures. I learned to surround myself with intelligent people, check my belief system, and to continue to learn and grow.

In December 2016, I celebrated 10 years of running my boutique investment firm A&O Aquisitions. It has been a rollercoaster, but what has stayed true and helped me grow are the basic principles I have mentioned above. The achievements and work I got to do in the past 10 Years blew my mind completely.

I like many quotes but two have been of great help to me. The first being "Whether you think you can or can't do something, you are right" by Ford. The other, by Theodore Roosevelt, which says, "It's far better to dare mighty things, to win glorious triumphs, even though checkered by failure... than to rank with those poor spirits who neither enjoy nor suffer much, because they live in a grey twilight that knows not victory nor defeat"

From them, I deduced that our thoughts and belief system paint our reality and our ability to change and shape our reality is down to us. I would also recommend James Allen's book, As a Man Thinketh.

I am interested in opportunities in Africa, and how I can contribute to developing the great continent, at the same time being able to build decent profitable companies. Technology and innovation has made the process enjoyable. Focus, hard work, and determination has made it achievable.

In 2014, in my Kitchen, I thought Nigerians should be able to trade in global markets using their local currency in real time. I looked for foreign partners to make the dream a reality and, in 2016, the dream came true. A lot went into it and it was a pleasure working with everyone to make it happen, but it is now a reality.

Success breeds more success, I have now learned how to dream bigger dreams. It has now become my favourite pastime. I have also learned how to wake up and act on the dreams as much as I possibly can. My thoughts and dreams have gotten much bigger and, funny enough, they don't scare me one bit but excite me.

My next stop is to build one of the largest financially inclusive companies Africa has ever seen, enabling everyone to invest across the continent with one single account. It's going to be one hell of a task and might take the rest of my lifetime to achieve it, but a long journey starts with little steps. I have taken the first one.

Gbite's ability to take many knocks and to keep failing forward, even with the many no's, has been one of the key determinants of his success, in addition to a possibilities mind-set.

Next is the story of a most admirable lady, who is recognised as the first lady of Mary Kay Cosmetics in the UK. I have known Elizabeth and her influential husband for over ten years. Her story and success is much recognised in London and the UK. Her self-discipline, entrepreneurial proclivity, superb sales ability, and big dreams have seen her achieve the very top spot in her company.

Below is her story:

ELIZABETH OZUA

Elizabeth Ozua is currently the first and number one Independent National Sales Director with Mary Kay Cosmetics UK Ltd., a direct sales company headquartered in Dallas, Texas. Mary Kay Cosmetics has a worldwide presence in more than 36 countries, founded by the legendary Mary Kay Ash in 1963.

Elizabeth reached the position of a National Sales Director, the highest position in the company, within 8 years of joining them. She is the first woman of African parentage to attain that position with Mary Kay Cosmetics Inc worldwide.

Elizabeth is the epitome of the Mary Kay Cosmetics dream. She began her career with this ground breaking company in September 1994 and she is celebrating her 23rd anniversary with the company this year 2017.

Prior to Mary Kay, she was a lecturer in a Nigerian University. She joined her husband, Peter, in the UK when he came for his specialist course in medicine. She took up a job in administration while doing various courses until she came across Mary Kay Cosmetics, which she started purely to supplement her income.

As her children were quite young, she wanted the flexibility of working from home. When she saw the potential and, as her income began to grow, she decided to commit her energies to the enterprise full time.

Elizabeth was very determined, and she encountered many testing challenges. She was undeterred because of the potential she saw with the Mary Kay business to earn some extra income. As she continued to overcome the challenges, she became even more successful. She enriches so many lives inside and outside Mary Kay.

She is constantly amazed at her success. For a business that started as something to earn a little bit of income on the side, it has grown so much with over 3000 people in her immediate Mary Kay National area. And these consultants that she works with are in different countries all over Europe and in the USA and Canada. She has made her mark in direct sales history through Mary Kay and still continues to do so. She is a great role model and a solid example of the rewards of hard work, determination and perseverance.

Elizabeth, who believes so much in the importance of discipline, focus, consistent commitment, perseverance, and bounce back ability, has been recognised in so many ways and forms because of her sterling work. She has been driving free for over 21 years with the famous Mary Kay car incentive.

This year, in 2017, the Mary Kay Company just delivered her 10th pink Mercedes, a lovely E Class. These are cars that she has earned to drive due to her sterling work and the excellent work of the team she is privileged to lead. In addition, she has also been rewarded with so many items of jewellery, gifts, holidays, and many other things. This lady understands that when you have a strong WHY, know your purpose and the reason why you are placed on this earth, then you go to work to make things happen.

She firmly believes that it is not where you start but where and how you finish that is important. She is always reminded that God had no time to make nobodies. We are all somebody. She suggests that we always dig deep and use our God-given talents to create our own worlds.

Elizabeth says that as you help people become successful, you in turn become successful, too. She has also been a useful asset to the Nigerians in Diaspora in the U.K. and many other communities in general.

She is happy to inform anyone who is willing to listen that, "Growth in any form or sphere doesn't just happen, any more than climbing a mountain just happens. You don't wander up a mountain and sur-prise yourself when you reach the top. Growth results from hard work."

She has been a keynote speaker on numerous occa-sions and at various events internationally and local-ly. She educates, coaches, mentors and shares good business practices on different platforms. This lady has helped so many through the charitable work that she does outside her business and continues to open new vistas.

The strategies that have enabled her to achieve so much through the vehicle of Mary Kay, in her own words, are:

1. **Changing Your Mind-set.** Train your mind and develop the confidence necessary to see things through challenging times.

2. **Get Rid of Negative Thoughts.** The greatest problem that plagues us and sabotages our effort is the negative thoughts we harbour that hold us hos-tage. You cannot drive forward using your rear view mirror as your guide.

3. **Persistence Pays.** Persistence is as a result of dis-cipline. Commitment means completion. The differ-ence between people who want to quit and successful people is perseverance. The key to success is to de-cide what is most important to you and take massive actions daily to improve on it.

4. **Always remember why you started a venture.** You had a dream, hope and a goal in mind. It doesn't change unless you change it.

5.   **There's Power in the Process.** Have Faith. Believe in yourself and your products. Keep learning and growing and never give up until the work is done.

6.   **Giving Back.** Always think of how you can give back. What you send into the lives of others, will inevitably come back to you.

7.   **Bounce Back Ability.** We all have problems, disappointments, and frustrations; however, it is how we deal with our setbacks that will shape our lives more than anything else we do. God's delays are not God's denials.

8.   **Surround Yourself With Like-Minded People.** This is most important. People who will lift you up when you are down and remind you of your dreams when they start to play hide and seek.

9.   **Focus on what you can do today.** Sometimes thinking too far ahead and overthinking things kill our dreams.

10. **Me Time.** Always remember to acknowledge yourself, appreciate yourself, forgive yourself and most importantly, to love yourself and those around you.

Elizabeth is determined to continue growing in direct sales with Mary Kay Cosmetics as her vehicle. She is so looking forward to the day when her company moves into Africa. Then, she can share with others in that continent what she has gained from the wonderful opportunity she has been so privileged to benefit immensely from.

Elizabeth is married to Chief (Dr) Peter Ozua and

they are blessed with 2 amazing children, Peter Junior and Assumpta Ozua. Both are very successful young adults in their chosen professions.

Chapter Nine:

Why You Must Develop Your Personal Leadership

"Leaders are people who define direction, inspire movements, and deliver pre-determined objectives"

-Charles Ajayi-Khiran

If everything rises and falls on leadership, according to leadership guru John Maxwell, then I believe it is incumbent on anyone looking to become an entrepreneur to understand this important subject. In this chapter, I want to discuss the role of your personal leadership to your entrepreneurial success.

I had the great experience of working many years ago as a senior executive consultant for the world's oldest career management company for mid– senior level executives in the city and west end of London. I was able to interview over 3000 senior executives who were in-between roles and seeking for other top positions. I worked with over 400 of these senior players over a six-year period to assist them in locating another position of either running a small, medium, or large company.

These individuals where not only Brits. Many came from right across Europe attracted to the vibrant London economy. For most, I observed first-hand the importance of superb leadership in many of them. I witnessed the absence of true leadership in some of them and how it affected their abilities to function at the highest levels.

Why is leadership important? Because true leadership is the ability to develop a vision that will motivate those you are leading to move with passion toward achieving a common goal with enthusiasm.

But first, let me begin by dealing with the importance of developing your personal leadership before discussing how to lead others. Before I do that though, I would like us to investigate some thoughts on leadership from great leadership authorities.

I encourage you to slowly go through the selection of leadership quotes I have assembled for you below, so the great truths they are articulating can be grasped and reflected on.

Here are 17 top quotes on leadership:

1. The late Professor Warren Bennis said; *"Leadership is a function of knowing yourself, having a vision that is well communicated, building trust among colleagues, and taking effective action to realize your own leadership potential".*

2. *"Leadership may be considered as the process (act) of influencing the activities of an organized group in its efforts towards goal-setting and goal achievement"* - Professor Ralph Stogdill

3. *"Leadership is influence, nothing more, nothing less"* - John Maxwell

4. *If your actions inspire others to dream more, learn more, do more, and become more, then you are a leader"* – John Quincy Adams (former US President)

5. *"it is not the position or rank that makes the leader, but the leader who makes the position"* - Stanley Huffy

6. *"Issuing orders is worth 10%. The remaining 90% consists of assuring proper rigorous execution of the order"* -- General George Patton

7. *"Also worth remembering is that in any man's dark hour, a pat on the back, and an earnest hand clasp, may well work a small miracle"*-General Marshall

8. *"He who thinks he leads, but has no followers, is only taking a walk"* --A leadership proverb

9. *"Leadership is a combination of character and strategy; if you were to do without one, do without strategy"* - General Norman Schwarzkopf

10. *"A crowd is a tribe without a leader"* – Seth Godin

11. *"The first responsibility of a leader is to define reality. The last is to say thank you. In between, the leader is a servant"* —Max DePree

12. *"A leader is a dealer in hope"* —Napoleon Bonaparte

13. *"Before you are a leader, success is all about growing yourself. When you become a leader, success is all about growing others"* —Jack Welch

14. *"A leader is one who knows the way, goes the way, and shows the way"* -John Maxwell

15. *"Effective leadership is not about making speeches or being liked; leadership is defined by results, not attributes"* —Peter Drucker

16. *"A leader takes people where they want to go. A great leader takes people where they don't necessarily want to go, but ought to be"*—Rosalynn Carter

17. *"It is absurd that a man should rule others, who cannot rule himself"* —   Latin Proverb

The above quotes provides lots to chew on regarding the subject of leadership. The various definitions and thoughts on the subject gives us an overall insight into this very important subject.

WHY LEADERSHIP IS ESSENTIAL

As an entrepreneur, you will likely go through different stages of business growth as your business matures. It is important to know what skills you will require at different stages of your evolution. Research has shown very few entrepreneurs were successful as leaders or CEO's of their enterprise once it grows large.

The right leadership will make everything work together seamlessly. Without leadership, all other business resources are ineffective. Leaders do not get it right every time, but they make better progress than those without leadership skills. Since everything rises and falls on the leader, it means without leaders nothing can really happen because there can be no mass action, no true accomplishments, no real conscience, definitely no profit, and, of course, the attraction of great talent will be missed.

Now, when you bear in mind that all successful endeavors are the result of human effort, it means your ability to influence others will be a derivation of the following:

- Your ability to articulate a clear vision in terms of direction.

- Your interpersonal skills/communications.

- How you manage conflict.

- How good you are at solving problems.

Here are some key areas to work on developing if you don't possess them already. These are very important while building your dream. By developing these areas, it will prevent you from sabotaging your own success now and in the future. The good news is that leaders are mainly made as opposed to being born, so anybody with the desire and commitment can become an outstanding leader.

There are many fine books, audio trainings and executive and corporate coaches that can help you develop your leadership skills. By understanding the subject of leadership and developing your own leadership, it will help accelerate your success.

8 IMPORTANT QUALITIES OR TRAITS TO DEVELOP FOR YOUR PERSONAL LEADERSHIP

1) Purpose/vision – this is an indispensable quality of a leader. The great Jack Welch says "Good business leaders create a vision, articulate the vision, passionately own the vision, and relentlessly drive it to completion." Developing and sustaining a vision bigger than you is critical to building a substantial enterprise. Your vision and purpose is what empowers you when things get difficult. Effective leaders know what they want to do, and have the strength of character to pursue their objectives in the face of opposition and in spite of failures. Having the strength and conviction to see your vision through is one of the most vital prerequisites of a solid leader.

2) Creativity – Many successful leaders have found creativity to be in the top three traits or qualities for outstanding leadership. This is due totally to the volatility and complex nature of today's global business landscape. IBM's 2010 Global CEO Study, which surveyed more than 1,500 chief executive officers from 60 countries and 33 industries worldwide, concluded that creativity is now the most important leadership quality for success in business. So creating something

unique, novel, and different in today's fast pace world is now key as businesses grow and fail so quickly like never before. Creativity and creative problem solving are now critical for entrepreneurs and business leaders to survive.

3) Integrity – when character is lost, all is lost. Integrity builds trust like nothing else. Keep your word. If you promise or say you are going to do something, then do it. If you forget, call or send a message to the person and apologise that you forgot to do whatever it was you promised to do. People lose respect very fast for people without integrity and it can seriously damage your reputation so that no amount of PR can fix it. Leaders must live by a higher standard than followers. What your people see you do, they believe. You must strive for moral uprightness and absolutes. If your people don't trust you, then you cannot get the best of them.

4) Values – The impact of this unconscious and invisible force is so important in your foundation as part of the truth you stand on. Your values make you strong and unshakable. What principles are important to you that are non- negotiable? Your values define not what you do but how you do what you do; this is the substratum of everything you do. For example, honesty, striving for excellence, winning, consistent, reliable, dependable, fun-loving, passionate, committed, respect for people regardless of their differences and treating them with dignity, are all examples of strong values.

5) Courage – As the great Sir Winston Churchill said *"Courage is the most important of human virtues, for upon it the others depend."* Aristotle equally said some-

thing similar he said *"courage is the first of human qualities because it's the quality that guarantees the others."*

Just think about it. Without courage, you will not even get off the starting line. You will not venture in the direction of your dreams and the idea will die a silent death. Courage enables you to take action in spite of the difficulties and uncertainty confronting you. As a matter of fact, true leadership starts from within the leader's heart, where true courage resides. As somebody once said, *"courage is fear that has said it's prayers."* Courage is not the absence of fear, but the ability to act in spite of the fear. And that is what leaders do, they act in spite of fear.

6) Decisive – when it comes to leadership, decisiveness is one of the most important traits. Can you just imagine a leader standing around, unclear and uncertain, confused and not knowing what to do? Solid leaders must know how to balance emotion with reason, and they must know how to make challenging decisions. That could be like knowing whether to make a move right now, or to wait, whether to fire somebody or re-assign them. Some experts say 75% of decisions need to be made right away, and for the bigger decisions, a deadline date must be set when the decision will be made which removes the stress from the situation. It is important to note here that leaders who are decisive do not necessarily get it right every time. However, they become better by sharpening their decision making ability as they practice it.

7) Confident – You must show and act confident in every situation you find yourself. If you think and act confidently, then you will be confident. Never publicly show your fear about any situation. Always put up

a confident attitude, because it automatically rubs off on your people. There were many times in the past when I found myself in difficult situations. Sometimes, the wrong information was passed out to the market which could have cost the company hundreds of thousands of pounds if we were to make refunds. Sometimes, the fate of the company in the particular market was at stake. I have had my top leadership calling me and telling me it was all over and they were not prepared to go to the field to make the announcements. They were waiting to hear what I had to say or what I wanted them to do about the very difficult situation. The first thing I did was to silence the fear. Then, I said a prayer for wisdom and strength to know what to do. Guess what? We survived it and calmed many nerves. Sometimes, we lost customers in the process. Privately, even if I had a measure of panic, I disguised it with confidence and positivity, and fortunately we always came out of the woods. Never show fear in front of your people. They draw energy from you.

8)   Focus - Focus is the extent to which you can concentrate without distractions on what must be done. As an entrepreneurial leader, this is important to your success and the success of your organisation. Daniel Goleman calls focus the hidden driver of excellence. In terms of the repertoire of attention, however, he said leaders need strength in three areas of focus: self (inner), people (other), and system (outer) awareness. Inner focus attunes us to our emotions and intuitions, guiding our values and helping us make better decisions. Other focus smooths our connections to the people in our lives. And outer focus lets us navigate the larger world.

Looking at the above 8 traits and qualities required for successful personal leadership, you can begin to understand why it is vital to develop these for your success. You can also observe why the lack of these traits are equally sabotaging so many entrepreneurs potential for success.

QUALITIES AND TRAITS TO DEVELOP FOR LEADING OTHERS

Now let us look at some of the very important qualities you will need for leading others effectively as your enterprise grows. Armed with some of the above personal leadership traits, here are some of the key attributes to develop for effective people leadership:

1) Communication – You have to treat communication as a vital process, just like you do marketing, sales, and profit generation. To inspire your team, you must learn to focus on mastering clarity and simplicity in your communication. Great leaders are effective communicators. If your people are not clear on what you are communicating, then there may be confusion right through the entire business.

As a matter of fact, many rank clear communication as the single most important quality of outstanding leadership. As General Colin Powell advises; "Leaders know that teams succeed when there is open and honest communication. They encourage creativity, innovation, and productivity by opening up communication channels between customer and service provider". If you think about it, there is really no mystery here.

Regardless of whether you're talking about business, sports, military or politics, the most successful leaders are brilliant communicators. Everyone is quickly aware of what their values are, and they live those values which command the admiration of their teams. Likewise, if you want your company to reach new and dizzying heights of effectiveness and success, you must master the art of clear communication.

2) Team building- The word team signifies synergy. It means the bringing together of a group of talented or like-minded people in a spirit of harmony to achieve specific goals or objectives. The essence of a team is their common commitment that binds them together, or else they are simply a group of individuals pursuing their own individual ends. Team building is one of the most important investments you can make as a leader.

According to a recent Forbes article, teambuilding builds trust, mitigates conflict, encourages communication, and increases collaboration. Effective team building means more engaged employees, which is good for your company culture and boosting of the bottom line. Remember, successful leaders all through history have been able to use their innate qualities to influence a team, workforce, or nation to achieve incredible goals.

Effective leaders combine their strengths, with the strengths of others to achieve impossible dreams. Some of the smartest leaders are those who intentionally seek to attract talented people to their employ who possess skills they don't have.

3) Delegation – As your business begins to grow, you may find yourself becoming overwhelmed by too many demands. The answer is definitely better delegation to others who will help do some of the heavy

lifting. Far too many leaders believe they are the only ones who can do the job just right.

I have fallen foul of this myself many times in the past until I learnt very valuable lessons. This is an error to think and act this way in leadership. The ability to wisely and effectively delegate is a quality far more discreet than others, and yet it is one of the most crucial to a leader's success. Whatever your business description, effective delegation is one of the keys to achieving your goals.

A person who insists on maintaining all control and authority is insecure and actually does not qualify for a description as a great leader. A leader is primarily an executive, a person who manages time, resources, and people. Finally, a leader who delegates increases the morale, confidence, and productivity of subordinates or followers.

4) Interpersonal skills – These are the special qualities that a Martin Luther King, Jr. or an Abraham Lincoln possess to make them paragons and proponents of inspiration in the hearts of multiplied millions of their ardent followers. Interpersonal skills are essentially goal-directed behaviours that we use in face-to-face interactions to achieve our desired outcomes and manage relationships more effectively. An effective leader must be well versed in the effective use of interpersonal skills.

In a 2005 poll by the Centre of Creative Leadership, it found an overwhelming 82% of those polled rated the ability to build relationships as the most important competency for success as a leader.

What special qualities did Martin Luther King, Jr.

or Abraham Lincoln possess to make them paragons and proponents of inspiration in the hearts of multiplied millions of their ardent followers? Interpersonal skills, the mixture of verbal and non-verbal communication, listening skills, team working, persuasion, negotiation and influencing skills to name but a few.

Here is the story of one of the most dynamic and effective leaders to be found anywhere in the world.

DAN HOLZMANN'S STORY

One of the most outstanding, successful, and powerful business leaders I know among the thousands I have had the pleasure of knowing or working with is my friend, Dan Holzmann. Dan exemplifies what I have just elucidated about the essence of leadership. Dan Holzmann is the President & CEO of The Juice PLUS+® Company Europe, based in Basel Switzerland.

I have known Dan for over 20 years. He is a most gracious and humble leader and one of the best people persons, and results-oriented leaders anywhere in the world. He has an infectious personality and a calm assurance about him that immediately puts people at rest.

Standing at 6' 4, handsome with piercing blue eyes, he utilizes to maximum effect bags of emotional intelligence in his dealings with his large corporate staff and tens of thousands of his distributors and customers. He is what I call a rousing leader, who possesses the rare skill of igniting his people and leading them toward huge, pre-determined corporate objectives. Under his stewardship, The Juice Plus+ company Europe has experienced some incredible growth, adding an average of 300-500 million dollars to the overall purse of the company.

Dan demonstrated his entrepreneurial spirit from a young age when he established Switzerland's first pizza home delivery outlet in 1989, at the tender age of 18. He followed that feat by establishing Switzerland's first airline broker in 1991, before joining Juice PLUS+® in 1993 as a master licensee for Juice PLUS+ in Europe. In 2012 Dan became one of the largest shareholders of The Juice PLUS+ company after playing an important role in merging the USA and EMEA businesses.

Dan's phenomenal success has not just been with Juice Plus. He continues to achieve great feats with the incredible skill of attracting some of the best people and building formidable partnerships with them. So many of his partners have become millionaires and multi-millionaires by locking arms with him and waging exciting and challenging wars.

Some of Dan's other outstanding achievements:

• President and founder of dh management ag, the management company of former world No.1 and 2008 French Open champion Ana Ivanovic.

• Dan is also a leading property developer. His luxury enclave in Kilchberg, Switzerland was named "The Best Place to Live in Switzerland"

• Dan also co-developed arguably the most coveted villas in Palma de Mallorca as the majority shareholder of Lions Ltd, a Spanish luxury developer.

• Dan is also a large shareholder of another Swiss

Property Group, a company with an active ambition of re-engineering the real estate industry in Switzerland.

DAN'S THOUGHTS ON OVERCOMING CHALLENGES

I actually get stronger when things don't go my way. I like crisis management. This is when I feel I can utilize a lot of my positive thinking, experience, and solution-oriented skills. During a period of "setback" I try to learn, to understand the mistakes we have made, and to make sure we don't repeat them again.

There have been so many! For example, I have had partners that were greedy and tried to push me out of the business. Very early in my business career, I had a partner who locked me out of the office because he was trying to take sole control of the company. I have been accustomed to drama and conflict from a young age.

I lost millions during my first year with Juice Plus+ as a master distributor. It's not easy to be instantly successful. It took me time to learn and improve, and to listen to as many experts as I could.

It's hardly an original thought, but I must emphasize the importance of teamwork. It is so, so hard to succeed on your own. And even if you do, it's not much fun. You want people around you to be able to celebrate with, and to enjoy each other's achievements.

HOW HE MAINTAINS SELF-BELIEF IN THE FACE OF UNCERTAINTY

I try to remember the good times and what success

felt like. I am prepared to do anything possible to get that feeling back.

HOW HE DEALS WITH REJECTION

I try to analyze why it happened and if I need to change. I adjust and try again until I am not rejected.

HOW HE DECIDES WHEN TO PULL THE PLUG ON A PROJECT OR VENTURE

I have never given up in business. In my private life, I have given up a few times. I will, however, pull the plug when I lose hope or motivation.

This can be due to a number of factors. I am also ready to pull the plug on a venture if there's a risk of adversely impacting the future of my team or business associates.

Dan lives in Zurich with his wife and three children. In his spare time, he loves to spend time with his kids, travel, and watch his beloved FC Basel.

CONCLUSION

Finally, I will leave you on this chapter with the immortal Mark Twain's quote on daring to be great! He said, *"Keep away from people who try to belittle your ambitions. Small people always do that, but the really great people make you feel that you, too can become great"*

Chapter Ten:

Learn To Employ
Yourself

"Job security is a myth. It's also risky for self-employed people, in my opinion. If they are sick, injured, or die, their income is directly impacted"
– Robert Kiyosaki

Many global and well-known businesses started either in a garage, kitchen, hallway, or bedroom. Many people worked at home before they made it and moved to external office space, and many more still operate a home-based business.

Since more and more entrepreneurs are now coming from a corporate environment, where they are used to structure and order, a large number are finding it difficult to be focused and effective working from home because of all the distractions.

If I have not mentioned it before, let me say it now that entrepreneurship without question will be one of the most difficult things you will ever do in your life. Entrepreneurship will totally consume you, and there will be many, many sacrifices to be made. Your children, if you have them, will suffer. Your spouse will suffer. Your relatives and friends will suffer from your absence and lack of attention.

You will be married to the business for a long time, no joking here, truly for real. My hard advice is, if possible, to resist getting married or having a family until you are afloat. Many marriages have ended in divorce because of the strain entrepreneurship has afflicted on the relationship either due to constant fights about insufficiency of money, or fights because of the lack of attention to your spouse or partner. This may be because you are either on the phone constantly, or out meeting people trying to create opportunity, or simply just trying to put food on the table.

The other big issue to contend with is the stress factor. When the business is haemorrhaging money due to the non-existence of cash flow, it is usual to be up most nights trying to figure out how to keep afloat. A lot of thinking and planning time goes into it. Your mood is affected as you are trying hard to figure out how to make this thing work. One moment you are celebrating a quick victory and popping open, Champagne thinking the good times are here, and the next moment you are wondering where the money has gone and if you should throw in the towel.

In my opinion, there are about a handful of the big ones that will really task you in life, and these are not in any particular order:

- Marriage and raising children

- Starting a business

- Moving premises

- Bereavement

- Divorce

Now, of course, there are different strokes for different folks. However, these are the big ones I have found personally and in my conversations with others. Starting a business is definitely in the top two as it literally consumes you.

For many people, they have been fortunate by achieving quick success. However, going by the statistics of over 80 per cent of businesses failing within the first 2-5 years, you begin to get the overall picture. So, it should not be a light-hearted decision to go into business.

Ensure you count the cost and find as many cushions as possible as back up. If you are able, ensure you have at least a minimum of 6 months savings behind you, unless you are fortunate enough to have generous bank loans or investors behind you.

YOU WILL NEED DISCIPLINE TO SUCCEED

Once you go into business for yourself, remember you are now your own boss. Nobody tells you what to do anymore, you are now in charge. You no longer work in the corporate world or for somebody else, where everything is planned in terms of when you get to work and when you finish.

A corporate or office environment gives you structure and discipline, people to socialise with, and your superiors to keep you on check and accountable etc. But now you don't have anyone who tells you when to go for your coffee or lunch breaks, or when you can take your holidays.

So without question, you are going to learn how to employ yourself and be effective so you can get work done. If you still have the pleasure of working from home, there are certain rules you would want to abide by so you don't spend all day watching television and making yourself 10 cups of tea or coffee.

If you do not put down some ground rules, the fact you are working at home, your spouse and children will take it for granted that you are home and won't respect the fact that you are actually working.

Here are some key things to do in order to create efficiency and have some measure of effectiveness:

1. Discipline yourself to wake up at a certain time daily, unless you are having a light or lazy day. This

will give your mind discipline and consistency.

2.   Get into the habit of creating a solid daily routine. Create a 'to do' list the night before so your mind has something to focus on overnight, or if you are an organised person, you can create one every morning.

This creates structure and focus even though your day may be interrupted by different things, some positive and others maybe not. If you do not have a list, there will be a tendency to fire fight all through the day, and it will make it more difficult to measure results.

3.   Do something for your mind so your mind in turn responds to you. Begin by reading or listening to something inspirational for 20 – 30 minutes at least every morning. It could be spiritual material like the Bible or other inspirational books.

When you regulate your mind this way, you fortify yourself against the myriad of things that will hit you on any given day. Plus, you will maintain an inspired or motivated state to achieve better results. Prayer or meditation is also a powerful and important thing to make a habit. Asking for a little help is not a bad idea at all.

4.   Next do something for your body. Now, there are plenty of things you can elect to do for your physical exercise. The key is to do something that you are able to maintain. If it is not possible to go to the gym, do something else you can be consistent in.

This could be a power walk or jogging for 30 minutes, or you can use a home exercise program. The old saying goes "if you don't feel well, you can't do well." You must work on your personal fitness, as entrepreneurship needs your mind and body in super shape.

5.   Avoid a heavy breakfast as it will make you sluggish and lethargic. Eggs are wonderful and healthy; oatmeal is also very good as it makes you feel full. Also you may want to try power juice or protein shakes with berries and seeds.

A strong cup of coffee will also create mental alertness because of the strong caffeine, if you are into coffee. Whatever works for you. The key point here is to avoid heavy breakfast as that will slow you down.

6.   Develop the habit of dressing up. This may be just putting on your jeans and a shirt and head to your home office at a particular time every day. I know some people who remain in their pyjamas and are still very effective. If that is you, then that is great.

For me, whenever I am working from home, I have to dress up and put on aftershave and switch on work mode before I hit the phones or computer in order to be effective. When you dress for work, it transmits a subliminal message to your subconscious that you are in work mode.

7.   Resist going into the kitchen every minute or hour, or going to play that video game and getting carried away. When it is time for you to take a break, do so. However, have a look at your to-do list and let it inform you how well you are making progress with the things you must accomplish for that day.

8.   If you break for lunch and have to watch a little news on television, do so, but keep your eyes on the

clock and know when to get back to your desk.

9.   If for any reason, your home is not conducive for work sometimes, find your favourite hotel where you can take your work and enjoy a calm atmosphere. Plus, you can meet your clients at the hotel, too.

10. Working from home is a great way to save on office costs, unless you are in a business where you have to employ lots of staff right away. Many people are running businesses with multi-million dollars or pounds turnover from their home office.

Technology has become so powerful that it is entirely possible to work from home without the daily commute to an office location. I worked from home for over 10 years successfully before having an external office, and I still use both to this day.

Chapter Eleven:

The Lonely
Seasons

"Entrepreneurship
is living a few years
of your life like
most people won't
so you can spend
the rest of your life
like most people
can't"
-*Anonymous*

Entrepreneurs are like eagles. They don't flock, and you find them one at a time. It is truly a lonely journey for entrepreneurs, because they are mostly going against the accepted norms of society. Society expects you to go to school and spend the rest of your life working a job.

Entrepreneurs, on the other hand, are people working according to their own dictates, hoping to take their dream to the world and hopefully live a great life from the proceeds of their enterprise.

It is however important to point out that it is not easy sailing. Your striving to succeed in your enterprise may sometimes feel like it is all in vain. Constantly remind yourself that you were created to solve a problem, and your work and success will take you to places where you will be constantly celebrated as the toast of the town or city. However, there is a price to pay for this success you crave! One of the biggest things to manage and discipline as an entrepreneur is your mind.

This sounds easier to say than doing it, but you must if you want to maintain your sanity. Entrepreneurship is not for the faint-hearted. As a matter of fact, I am constantly amazed why anyone in their right minds would want to go into entrepreneurship! Then I ask myself, what is the alternative?

Seriously though, anybody who has ever built a business will tell you the constant high and lows they are acquainted with. You will definitely have to find ways of keeping your mind positively engaged or else it will create plenty of opportunities for you to worry and doubt.

You have probably heard it said that it is lonely at the top, especially when you are the owner or CEO. That is not a lie. It is truly lonely at the top! You see, for some time you alone carry your dream and your ideas in your mind. You alone give it life and expression.

Some of your successes you tend to share, but many of your failures and disappointments you don't usually express or share with people. You carry them alone in your mind.

Entrepreneurship is about trying out new things, about innovating, about re-presenting an idea, service, or product back into the market. It is about persuading and changing the minds of people, helping them to see things in another or a better way. Many of the time you are only left with your own deep thoughts for company as you fully engage in trying out new things, searching for new buyers or customers, willing for that telephone to ring with some good news.

As much as doubts can be one of the meanest punishers constantly harassing us, it can also act as our checks and balances. Doubts make us question things we would otherwise take for granted. It makes us evaluate everything with scientific rigour.

Loneliness can be very deadly, especially when you have no support from the closest people to you, as you do not want to mention another disappointment to your nearest and dearest. If you do, they may start complaining again that you should go and get a job like everyone else or remind you of the accumulating bills that require desperate attention.

A time comes when you stop sharing with your spouse or partner because they have heard all your reasons before. They usually begin to give you that look that they understand, but you know they have really had enough. They are really just trying not to say the wrong things to you.

Instead, they are silent and give you that knowing look, more like smiles of sadness and frustration and even sometimes pity, as they question your sanity. This begins to really affect your morale as you now begin to doubt yourself and wonder if the opportunity, business or product is truly worth it.

However, there is something deep inside you that keeps reassuring you not to give up, that you are close to success, that in maybe just one more month, just one more year, and then it becomes two, three, five years and you are still not out of the woods yet. Now, hope is all but finally gone and you are holding on purely by a thread.

For many, it is crash time, as you run out of steam, out of money, out of patience and excuses, and frustration and anger sets in. During these dark periods, you may find yourself getting lonelier and lonelier, alone with your worries and doubts, fearful of what the future holds. You may wonder whether there will ever be more to life than your current realities.

For some fortunate people, they may not have to struggle for that long before they are out of the woods as the business takes off through whatever means. For most others, as the various statistics show, due to a myriad of reasons, they crash and their business does not make it. Now they have to start thinking or wondering what to do to put bread on the table.

It is at this time that they go out to buy newspapers, check the internet, and start looking for something to support them for the moment before attempting another go at entrepreneurship for the die-hard entrepreneurial types. They search for work in sales, selling windows, insurance, or anything to bring in reasonable money. Some seek part-time work in stores, or use their contacts to find something, anything, at this time to bring in money. Others retrain for another career while still harbouring hopes of fighting another day after healing from the bruises of the failure.

Some who have driver's licences look into driving as a chauffeur or for Uber. Some take construction work. The list is endless, all seeking temporary means of bringing in some money, as they contemplate what to do next.

DIFFERENTIATING LONELINESS FROM SOLITUDE

One of the key practices of leaders is solitude, because as leaders there is much time required for reflecting, planning, and strategizing. Entrepreneurs must also cultivate this excellent habit. While everyone is sleeping or partying, leaders are awake thinking and planning for the welfare and wellbeing of all the people partying and sleeping. However, solitude is completely different from loneliness, and we will look at some of the differences next.

There is a great quote by Hannah Arendt, one of the most famous political philosophers of the 20th century, she said the difference between solitude and loneliness is as follows:

"The lonely man finds himself surrounded by others with whom he cannot establish contact or to whose hostility he is exposed. The solitary man, on the contrary, is alone and therefore can be together with himself"

That is so beautifully articulated by Hannah.

So here are some thoughts and differences between solitude and loneliness:

SOLITUDE

•   Solitude, for most intents and purposes, is enlightened choice, a strategic separation from people and noise for a specific and wholesome purpose.

•   Solitude can be a powerful positive state.

•   Solitude allows for deep introspective analysis and re-evaluation. There is much power available in solitude as the mind is able to reflect.

•   Solitude allows you to get in touch with your inner man, and receive wisdom and instruction on what next steps to take.

•   Solitude allows you to re-energise and recharge your batteries.

LONELINESS

•   Loneliness, on the other hand, is unhealthy because it connotes sadness, isolation, lack of friends and companions.

•   You can be lonely in the midst of people, even supposedly loved ones.

•   Loneliness can feel like punishment, it can be

caused by self-inadequacy.

• If you are not careful, the negative state of loneliness can lead to self- hate.

• Loneliness is the feeling of absence, like something is missing in your life, and this could be a temporary loss of purpose or a loss of confidence.

• Everyone, not only entrepreneurs, experience s loneliness at some point in their lives

Some people call loneliness the silent killer. It has been shown to elevate vastly a person's risk of heart disease, stroke, and cancer according to research by the University of North Carolina. Also, to reiterate, people who find facing challenges alone a great bother may not be cut out for the life of an entrepreneur.

Here is some advice from my own experience and from that of other individuals I have spoken with on this subject.

- Get a mentor and speak to him or her constantly, or at least once a week. Ask if you could see your mentor once a week or fortnight and buy lunch for him or her. You should usually feel energised whenever you spend time with a great mentor.

- Invest in a hobby, something outside your work, if you don't already have one. Take up boxing lessons, running, golf, tennis, cooking, hiking, photography, parachuting, cycling etc. Find something you like and join and meet other people.

- Learn to network with others. Attend social events or business clubs and mix with real people every so often. This will help stave off loneliness.

- Focus on the reason why you started your business. Is it to educate your children in great schools? Is it for financial freedom or any other reason? Focus on those during down times.

- Get involved with other things besides yourself. Focus on others, volunteer your time to charities, or your church. This usually gets your mind focused on the bigger and more important things of life than your own personal issues.

SO IS ENTREPRENEURSHIP WORTH ALL THE TROUBLE?

Since entrepreneurship, as we have discoursed in some length, is full of risks, depending on your line of business and since your mental health and personal finances can also be at risk, is it really worth it?

One of the best pieces of advice I can give you is to try to enjoy the journey itself, and not focus only on the destination. The truth is that many entrepreneurs, as mentioned before, never make it big. True success is indeed rare for entrepreneurs, and that is a fact!

Many dream of the wealth and power entrepreneurship may provide, but it just may never happen! So do the most with your opportunity and learn all the lessons and skills, as much as you can, along the way.

So here are my thoughts of whether it is all worth it to be an entrepreneur? Some benefits of being an entrepreneur:

1. You are your own boss and don't have to answer

to anyone for the most part. Also, you get to select and build your own team.

2.   You have the power to create your future and create your own destiny. As it has been said, the best way to predict the future is to create it.

3.   You are able to witness your concept, whether product or service, impact lives and you take ownership of the success.

4.   You have the satisfaction of adding value to the economy by creating jobs and becoming a respected business leader.

5.   Entrepreneurship may accord you with freedom and a jet set lifestyle, the opportunity to travel and visit many interesting cities and hotels.

6.   Great flexibility can be achieved with entrepreneurship. You get to choose where you work, either from the office, hotel lobbies, home, or beach.

7.   You could get really rich. If and when your business succeeds and begins to bring in huge profits, you could become very rich, influential and powerful.

8.   You could build generational business and wealth. By owning your own business, you have the opportunity to create generational impact. Something to pass down to your children's children if successful.

9.   Opportunities for huge growth and release of your potential. Entrepreneurship allows you to unveil what you are carrying within you. Because you are constantly learning and finding a way to break through, and do things better, you become much

more than you dreamt possible.

10. Variety. No day is ever the same. You are either dealing with new challenges, or celebrating new victories. Many entrepreneurs would not exchange this for a mundane 9 − 5 reality.

Chapter Twelve:

Failure Is Never
Final Until...

"Failure should be our teacher, not our under-taker. Failure is delay not defeat. It is a temporary detour, not a dead end. Failure is something we can avoid only by saying nothing, doing nothing, and becoming nothing"
–Denis Waitley

The Chinese multi-billionaire, Jack Ma, the founder & CEO of the behemoth tech company Alibaba, has a story that undoubtedly must rank as one of the most gripping portraits of uncommon persistence, determination and failures in recent history. His story is truly an inspirational account of the power and resiliency of the human spirit, and the miracles that can occur if we do not give up and keep trying.

Jack Ma's attitude toward failure is like no other. This 53-year-old business magnate essentially rose from nothing to one of the world's richest men in a meteoric fashion by learning quickly and never giving up.

Jack basically failed at everything he tried. Nobody would have bet a dollar on him succeeding against all the odds, but he believed in himself and defied the entire world with his stunning success. He was the kid in school whom many would have labelled stupid, as he failed literally all his tests.

According to him, he failed a key primary school test two times, he failed the test to get into middle school three times, and he also failed the test to get into college two times. Later, Jack attempted to enroll in the prestigious Harvard University, but there was a small problem. Harvard did not want him.

He did not give up, and tried 10 times to get into the Ivy League institution. Ten times they said no and rejected him. Jack was rejected from three universities, until he finally attended and graduated from Hangzhou Normal University.

He consequently applied for 30 different jobs but did not succeed in landing any of them. One of the jobs was with the famous chicken fast food restaurant, KFC. 24 people applied for the job and 23 were selected, but Jack failed the interview. Then he tried to apply for a job as a policeman. Out of the 5 people who applied, four got the job. He did not.

This highly inspirational history maker always had a way of talking to himself and reasoning away different disappointments. When he failed at the various jobs, he kept telling himself that it must be because he was not good looking and because he was short of stature. Even his wife attested to this when she said the reason she fell in love with him and married him was that even though he was not handsome, he could do lots of things most handsome men could not do.

Jack recorded so many more failures in business before his explosive rise to the very top. Today, everyone knows his name. However, if not for his perseverance and refusing to take no for an answer, the world probable would never have heard of him.

Today, he is China's richest man, worth approximately US$31.3 billion. He is ranked number 18 in the world's richest list, according to Forbes. Jack's company, The Alibaba Holdings Group, went public in 2014 with an initial public offering of $25 billion, making it the largest IPO in history.

The entrepreneurial world is littered with many failures, many disappointments. and many genuine frustrations. To become a truly outstanding entrepreneur, you have to constantly reinvent yourself. This is one of the reasons I wrote this book.

I wanted it to be a helpful and understanding companion, to give a true taste of what entrepreneurs go through, because everything you want is on the other side of failure. So begin now to get acquainted with failure. Do not ever fear failure, because it is a critical step to great success.

You cannot learn anything great or become anything special without failing. Failing is not a bad word. The only time you really fail and become stigmatized as a failure is when you refuse to get back up and you stop trying.

WILSON OLAYINKA'S STORY

My dear friend, Wilson, is undoubtedly a man with an unquenchable spirit, who has registered many failures and losses in his entrepreneurial campaigns. Below, he recounts part of his stunning story in his own words:

In December 2006, I was out jogging at 5am on a very cold winter's morning. I was sweating profusely in the cold. This was the day after everything had gone wrong. My business had irretrievably collapsed around me.

I had been successfully operating a money transfer business for the previous five years. The business employed twenty full-time staff members. We had over two hundred agencies in the UK, 150 in the Republic of Ireland, several in Germany, and were well-represented in New Zealand. We also had expansive payment outlets in Nigeria with a turn- over of a billion naira annually (USD\$7.5million). This was definitely a winter of discontent.

The night before was a difficult and sleepless one as I lay on my bed gazing at the ceiling with all sorts of frightening thoughts running through my mind. Like, "how did I get myself in this quagmire?" and "what will people say?" and "How do I sustain my family?" and,

What on earth am I going to do now, having virtually no penny in my account, but instead a large deficit?"

The first answer to all these questions that came to me loud and clear was, "It's not what happened to you, but rather what are you going to do about it that is more important." There and then, I got up and went jogging on that cold winter morning without really knowing yet what I was going to do about my predicament.

However, hope soon kicked in as I knew I would survive this horrendous experience. I had survived other serious challenges in my life up to this point, however, I had to admit this was proving to be the biggest fall so far. As hope came, my strength increased as I pictured in my mind's eye that "I could do it all over again; I can be successful in whatever I do, as long as I have the idea." Meaning, I have to bring my creativity to the forefront of my situation. However, my mind was still blank at this stage.

When I got back home post my jogging, I took a shower and went to our office in Newbridge, Ireland. The office was always filled with staff, and buzzing with customers waiting for the attention of the customer service representatives. The telephones that used to ring literally every minute seeking attention had now fallen silent, and the whole place was like a ghost town, deathly quiet.

I didn't quite know why I went to the office, putting on my smart and sharp looking charcoal suit. Getting there, I brought out the vacuum cleaner and cleaned the entire two story office building. When I finished, I brought out a blank sheet of paper which I still have to this day and wrote down the following:

1.   What is the most basic thing I must do right now to feed my family and service my most important bills?

2.   How do I connect with my creditors to let them know my predicament?

3.   What can't be cured immediately must be endured.

Before 12pm on this faithful and most difficult day, I decided to go out to find a static security job. After various enquiries, I found out I could earn approximately €400 per week, a huge reduction from my previous 6 figure income, but I could meet my most important and immediate commitments. With this in mind, the clock started ticking all over again as I knew without providing food for the family and roof over our heads, my mind cannot be creative.

I packed up my table, removed my tie and jacket, and went straight to a security company not too far from the house after securing an interview. That same night I started a security job at a local county council.

One of my discoveries in overcoming adversity is dealing with the "Now Situation" first and foremost before seeking answers to what went wrong. Once my mind was settled a bit, I could begin to think again and look towards the future with anticipation, as opposed to apprehension, as Tony Robbin's and Jim Rohn taught. Next is to plan ahead, matching the planning with equal amounts of dedication and discipline to create the right results again. Another thing I discovered is that ideas truly can be life changing if acted upon.

It was at my desk as a security guard right here in Ireland that I got the inspiration (idea) to start the first online shopping mall to Nigeria. This idea was instrumental in opening other big doors of opportunities.

It was also at my security desk protecting buildings and watching the CCTV cameras that ideas and opportunities came to me. These opportunities enabled me to foster a relationship with Travelex Money Transfer as their Master Agent in both United Kingdom and Republic of Ireland, which again opened more strategic and important doors.

It was also at this same desk that I forged a relationship with the Managing Director of Q-Card Master card to take Master card to Nigeria.

A very important point that I would like to reiterate is that the "People around you, and their belief in you, really counts"! During this dark period of my life which I call the 'winter of discontent', I was fortunate to have around me two people that were strong encouragers and constantly affirmed their belief in me that I could build it all again.

If I were to list in quick succession the reasons I did not completely sink in the quagmire of despondency when disaster struck, would be these:

1. My strong faith in God, and knowing He would

not leave me without support.

2.   Refusing to allow the problems to become my sole focus.

3.   The ability to deal with now and not worry about what people around me will say settling for a security job.

4.   Not focusing strictly only on the now, but looking to the future with a lot of anticipation.

5.   Coming up with creative ideas and pursuing the ideas with vigour.

6.   Remembering not to despise small beginnings, and not being afraid to start all over again.

Having learnt from the vicissitudes of life and business, with God on my side, I have been able to surmount them all with greater wisdom.

I am currently a very successful, professional Forex Trader and trainer, teaching many people strategies to generate as little as €200 daily in income and with associates in 6 countries. I am also a leadership trainer and speaker with affinity for software consulting for large corporations.

10 years on, we have made it again to the top with several business interests, and an enviable lifestyle. However, my greatest joy is passing all that knowledge on and transforming many lives one day at a time.

<u>SOME GREAT FAILURES CHANGING THE WORLD</u>

Thomas Edison, the great inventor, failed over

10,000 times trying to create a commercially viable electric light bulb, but did not give up until he succeeded. Colonel Harland Sanders, at the age of 62 with his $105 social security check in hand, went pitching his chicken recipe and was rejected over 1000 times, before founding the finger licking world famous Kentucky Fried Chicken. These two men are probably the two best examples used world over whenever it comes to conversations regarding great failures and dogged perseverance.

However, there are so many more with incredible failure stories before any eventual success. The truth is that life's best lessons are not found in your successes, but in your failures.

Let me make a very loud announcement to you now, so you do not think I crept up behind you and took you by surprise, You are going to fail in business, just as you will fail in life! Now there. We got that out of the way and you have heard me loud and clear. Let us now turn our attention to 10 famous failures changing and impacting our world:

1.   Arianna Huffington author and co-founder of The Huffington Post, is world famous, but she wasn't always. Before launching The Huffington Post, Arianna Huffington had a bit more trouble getting people to read her work. Her second book was rejected by 36 publishers. (Yes, you read that correctly — 36.)

2.   Multi-billionaire Jeff Bezos, founder of Amazon, is one of the biggest success stories of the online era. But before Amazon became a household name, the company's CEO had several failed ideas. One of the most notable was an online auction site, which evolved into zShops, a brand that ultimately failed.

Still, CEO Jeff Bezos would repurpose the idea into what would eventually become the Amazon Marketplace.

3.   Billionaire Larry Ellison, founder of the mighty Oracle, has had his share of ups and downs. After Ellison dropped out of college and worked as a programmer for eight years, he co-founded the company with his former boss. But Oracle struggled for years before making it big. Ellison even had to mortgage his house to obtain a line of credit to keep the business afloat during that time.

4.   Vera Wang, the famous fashion designer, has built a billion dollar fashion empire. However, she wasn't always known for her high-end wedding gowns. In fact, Wang was once a figure skater, but she failed to make the U.S. Olympic figure skating team. She then moved on to work for Vogue, but was turned down for the editor-in-chief position before leaving to become a designer.

5.   Billionaire Sir James Dyson, now one of Britain's richest men, wasn't always a well-known name associated with vacuum cleaners. In fact, it took Sir James Dyson 15 years and all of his savings to develop a bagless prototype that worked. He developed 5,126 prototypes that failed first.

6.   Billionaire Sir Richard Branson founded Virgin Atlantic in 1984, flying with one jumbo jet for a year. During the Government certification flight, birds flew into an uninsured engine, resulting in an explosion. Branson had to pull out cash from his overseas financial subsidiaries and reconstruct the company. After a court battle with British Airways and rising fuel prices,

plus the terrible economic environment of the 1990s, Branson sold off Virgin Music in 1992 to Thorn EMI. It has been a very rough path; but today, he is world famous and one of the 20 richest men in Britain.

7.   Veteran and iconic actor Sydney Poitier first auditioned for the American Negro Theatre, but flubbed his lines and spoke in a heavy Caribbean accent. The director angrily told him to stop wasting his time and go get a job as a dishwasher. But Poitier worked on his craft and eventually became a hugely successful Hollywood star. He won an Academy Award for Best Actor ("Lillies of the Field," 1963) and helped break down the colour barrier in the American film industry.

8.   The mega star Jay-Z could not get any record label to sign him. Growing up in the Marcy Projects in Brooklyn, Jay-Z worked to perfect his flow, his lyrics, and his references. When he couldn't get a single bite on his first CD, he and his friends sold the record out of the boot of their car. Now besides his music, he is also a major entrepreneur worth $550 million, according to Forbes.

9.   JK Rowling may be rolling in a lot of Harry Potter money today, but before hitting the jackpot with her Harry Potter series, she was nearly penniless, severely depressed, divorced, and trying to raise a child on her own while attending school and writing a novel. Rowling went from depending on welfare to survive to becoming one of the richest women in the world in a span of only five years through her hard work and determination.

10. Michael Jordan is an icon and perhaps one of

the greatest basketball players of all time. However, he was dropped from his high school team. Luckily, Jordan didn't let this setback stop him from playing the game and he has stated, *"I have missed more than 9,000 shots in my career. I have lost almost 300 games. On 26 occasions I have been entrusted to take the game winning shot, and I missed. I have failed over and over and over again in my life. And that is why I succeed."*

LESSONS FROM MY FAILURE

I speak as somebody who has experienced devastating failures in life. I still remember one of my most painful failures with much sadness. This was in the year 2001, when the sales and marketing business in the huge and emerging health and wellness space I had painstakingly built from the previous eight years collapsed.

I had registered some great successes and built a strong distributor base in 7 countries with nearly 10,000 people in it, many of them wonderful leaders and friends in the business. I was married to an ex-model and fashion designer. I enjoyed some of the finer things in life, strong cash flow, tailored suits, and lots of travel. Then, for no reason I could attribute to myself, the business began to go downhill in a very short space of time because of problems with the parent American company. This business had been good to me, paying me six figure incomes after a few years of developing it, and I was living the life of a star.

Then, suddenly and without warning, my income dropped from five figures monthly to three figures in the space of under 3 months. I tried really hard for about 18 months to rebuild it, but it just wasn't happening. My savings was disappearing fast, to the point that I had to go get a part- time job. I ended up losing literally everything.

My marriage packed up, my business packed up, and my health was greatly affected. I was diagnosed with high blood pressure and type 2 diabetes, I had very tiny boils on my head and I had to be on medication to bring down the high readings registering on my blood pressure.

I remember my wonderful doctor, then very concerned, who had a stern conversation with me. She told me that for a young man of 34 years I was in a very dangerous place. Anyhow, I thought my world was over. In truth, it took me a few years to recover before I fell in love again and married my current wife who was simply amazing and supportive during those turbulent and difficult years.

I understand and can really empathise with failing and failing big. Since then I have experienced more failures again, and some very painful, so when I write about this very difficult subject, please understand I really know what you are going through if you are experiencing or have experienced failures.

How could I in truth be an advisor to a billionaire today? How could I provide training for so many governments and corporations today? How could I support so many executives and royalty through Bespoke Coaching if I did not go through such difficult lessons and experiences?

Now please don't misunderstand me, I am not saying for you to run a successful training, speaking, and coaching practice like I do you have to go through a similar journey like mine. Each of us will go through our own path that life carves out for us. This just happens to be my story. However, look at me now. I have come out of it all stronger, wiser, and more successful than ever.

THE SUCCESSFUL MIND-SET

Let me tell you this, and it is the absolute truth, you are going to fail as long as you are trying to achieve something worthwhile. Failing is not a bad word or a disease. There are many times you are going to have to start all over in something. Life will test you and throw stuff your way that you will scream and cry that you do not deserve. And maybe you did not deserve it, but it is still going to happen to you.

Look, every successful entrepreneur has had to start all over many times. If you have not really failed yet, just wait. It is coming. Even if, like me, you built some amazing high-level contacts who throw significant business your way, some of those contacts may themselves get in trouble and become publicly disgraced as their organisations and banks got into serious trouble.

I watched powerful contacts disappear in a lightening short space of time. These were people whose patronage I enjoyed, and I hit a famine. I did not see it coming, and so it was back to the drawing board. I had about two years of very dry times until I was able to re-establish myself again. Having well-developed relationship building skills will definitely serve you well.

It does not really matter how many times you shout 'failure is not an option,' you will fail many times. As a matter of fact that phrase "Failure is not an option," was first made famous by Jerry C. Bostick, a NASA flight controller, when they were attempting to bring the damaged Apollo 13 back to Earth. In such precarious circumstances, one could understand why failure could not be an option.

Many deem failure a terrible deficiency, but that is not completely true. Why? Because your failure and defeat will be your greatest teachers as long as you learn from them! Everyone is teaching you how to develop a successful mind-set, which is great, but very few teachers show you how to deal with, manage, or succeed from failure.

Just think where we will be today if all those great failures and thinkers gave up? We may not be enjoying the sophistication of running water in our homes. We may have been condemned to drawing water out of wells and then transporting it back home in buckets. We would have equally been condemned to using torch or candle light and not experience the power and superior convenience of electricity. Our thanks forever goes to the great failure Edison.

Now, try and imagine a world without telephones. What about jet travel, which enables us to cut down unbelievable hours, days, and months from our travel time as we make mincemeat of thousands of miles, making it possible to get to our destination with panache?

How would we have been able to understand gravity if it were not for the great failure Sir Isaac Newton as he was taxing his brains about the forces of nature? How on earth could we have had access to one of the world's greatest inventions- the internet and portable computers- if it were not for great failures who attempted and failed repeatedly?

And when we are stressed, we have the high privilege of being entertained by some of the most amazing sports people like Michael Jordan, Ronaldo, Serena Williams, Federer, Anthony Joshua, and the other multitude of sports people who make us forget our temporary sorrows and problems as we laugh, cry, scream for joy and excitement as they dazzle us with their skills honed from deep failures?

What about the untold number of musicians who have given us some of the most enchanting music? What about actors and performances that brings both tears to our eyes and laughter to nourish our souls, honed from innumerable failures with so many of them who had to pick themselves up and dust their pants and go again?

How grateful are we for those great failures who gave us the convenience and comfort of travelling by motor cars instead of camels, donkeys, and horses? Not to even think about the geniuses who discovered powerful vaccines to treat deadly diseases, create precision surgical tools, provide artificial limbs to people without limbs? What about the great failures who refused to give up in their campaign against injustice and inequality?

Some spent a large part of their lives locked behind bars and some were even killed in the process! What great failures they were. The list is clearly endless, but I believe you get the picture. You want to know something else? All those examples I just mentioned were all developed, created, or performed by guess what? Big failures!!

There is only one distinction that separates them from genuine failures: the fact that they refused to give up. They kept getting up over and over again and dictating failure on their own terms. They decided what failure is. So it is entirely up to you, because the true definition of failure is somebody who gives up trying and refuses to get right back up! Question is? Are you a failure or you just failed in something temporarily? You answer.

Finally, remind yourself of what the late and immortal Jim Rohn taught. Jim was recognised as America's foremost business philosopher. He said when he was speaking about resolve - *"Resolve says I will. The man says, 'I will climb this mountain even though they told me it is too high, too far, too difficult. But it is my mountain, and I will climb it. You will soon see me waving from the top having conquered it, or dead on the side trying to climb it. But I am not coming back."*

Of course no one is asking you to die in the process, but you have to make a decision to go all out after your dreams. And as General Hannibal said, *"You either find a way, or make one."*

Chapter Thirteen:

Go The
Extra Mile

"If a person
compels you to
go a mile, go
two instead"
-Jesus Christ of Nazareth

Richard Ejiro Obahor is the CEO of Purple Premium Real Estate. He is a very successful London based property developer who specialises in luxury accommodations. He invited me to lunch at the exclusive Ritz hotel near Piccadilly Circus. The Ritz is a grand symbol of high society and luxury, and truly one of the most prestigious and best known hotels in the world.

Today, Richard enjoys the finer things of life, a testament to what uncommon service and dedication can provide founded on the substratum of high integrity. Below is his story in his own words, and how attention to service excellence and integrity has opened unusual doors for him and taken him to the very top of his profession. There are some important lessons to be gleaned from Richard's story.

RICHARD EJIRO OBAHOR'S STORY IN HIS OWN WORDS

First, let me begin by saying that I believe accomplishment, success, and achievements in general are a function of simple and well-applied principles. I am not a huge proponent of complex processes or methodologies. These are the principles below that I have applied right through my career that have generated the notable successes that I have recorded to date.

I bought my first property about 12 years ago and, like most people, I realised that I had some equity in it. So, I refinanced, and bought another property, refinanced and bought another one, and another one, and another one, and another one, until I managed to build a multi-million pound property portfolio in less than 2 years. At that point, I realized that I had some unique acquisition skills and I thought perhaps I could offer this as a service and charge people a fee for helping them to buy property.

That went well and soon after, because I knew there was more to be achieved, I decided to seek out foreign investors, especially in Nigeria, with intentions to invest in the UK. My dealings with most of these high net worth clients saw me going backwards and forwards to Nigeria, and they would invite me to their expensive and truly palatial mansions in Nigeria.

These mansions had very nice décor, but I was always able to see beyond the grandeur because of my knowledge of properties. I remember as I observed the properties, the defects would suddenly jump at me, and I would see the poor finish and workmanship in those beautiful homes. Either the walls where not smooth, or the tiles were wonky, or some other major defect would be seen. There was very poor workmanship in Nigeria.

I quickly spotted a gap in the market as I realised that I could transfer the skills and expertise that I gathered over the years in the UK and put it to use in building good quality homes in Nigeria. With that in mind, we launched our building project and have been really successful as we have only recently sold out our last development in Nigeria. We are also currently in the middle of a multi-million pound building project.

Our vision is to build 2022 homes right across Nigeria, Ghana, Sierra Leone, and Kenya by the year 2022, to house Africans living in the Diaspora. Overall, I would say I have not done too badly. I have had very influential people as my clients, including a President and one of the ten richest men in Africa, I have my own publication and have won a number of industry leading awards.

THE RECESSION

Things have not always been very rosy for me. Between 2009 and 2010 as a result of the recession, I lost everything. I went from driving a £40,000 car to a position where a friend had to loan me a car. I went from employing people to working in a recycling centre. I went from a £250K per year income to about £7 per hour income. It was a very devastating period.

However, I am indeed grateful, because within a very short space of time I was able to bounce back to the top of my game. This is very vital to my life story because after all the episodes, I knew there were lessons to learn. One crucial question I asked myself was this: Was I twice lucky, or is there anything peculiar that I could identify and share with others as my game changer, or the reason I won twice?

MY GAME CHANGERS

Integrity and Trust

I learnt very quickly the importance of integrity, and why I cannot do without it. The unfortunate thing is that integrity seems to have lost its meaning. People have no idea the powerful doors that integrity can open, and equally the doors that lack of integrity can shut. I mentioned earlier that I had a past president and one of the ten richest men in Africa as a client. These wealthy guys didn't respond to my marketing campaign, neither did I get to meet them because of my education, or my expertise, it was purely my integrity that opened these powerful doors, and someone else's lack of it.

Someone actually introduced me to these super rich individuals. I started working with a client about 5 years ago, a very wealthy chap. I helped him acquire a property here in the UK and we have since been working closely together. I have earned a small fortune working with this guy in return for the services I provided. A short while after we commenced our relationship, he got an appointment to work with the president of Nigeria, so he moved to Abuja the capital city. Through a series of events I was fortunate enough to be introduced to the President and his family and many more people. But the moral of the story is this.

One day, this gentleman and I were having a conversation. He recounted how six years earlier before we met, that he was introduced to another guy who was in a similar line of business to me. He told me then that he was planning a holiday to the UK with his family and asked this other guy to assist him in securing a nice short-let accommodation.

The chap then informed him that he had found a nice short-let accommodation for £6000. He continued with the story that he promptly sent the money over to the chap, but instead, the man arranged with another friend who lived in a flat, to vacate the flat and to rent his friend's flat to the client and his family.

This wealthy client would normally stay in a 5-star central London hotel, but instead found himself in this flat. He continued that the moment he arrived at the address, he realised the grand scheme that crooked chap had conceived. He did not even bother getting out of the car with his family. They went and checked into a hotel, and he never engaged with the chap ever again.

The sad thing in all of this is because the chap failed to operate with integrity, and thought £6000 was a lot of money, without realising it, he had just short changed his destiny. The chap lost out on hundreds of thousands worth of good business, and not to even speak of the influence and high net worth clients he would have been fortunate to know.

He lost all that for £6000, because of his lack of integrity! So, Richard attests, the crooked man's lack of integrity has been his gain.

I Conquered Fear

I strongly believe that you have to be fearless. As an entrepreneur I think this is quite important. I noticed that once I could conquer my fear, my eyes began to open to lots of opportunities. I remember I once bought a property a couple of years ago somewhere in Grimsby. I bought this property for £20,000, but it was one of those that I didn't actually go and visit before I bought it.

On the day I went to see the property the locals advised me that the location was wrong. Apparently, it was drug-ridden. The property, being empty and dilapidated, was their base.

Unfortunately, there was nothing I could do to reverse the purchase, so I had no choice but to proceed with the refurbishment. I spent around £20,000 on the project and I even employed some of the locals to assist with the refurbishment. In total, I spent approximately £40,000 and we ended up with a property valued at £120,000 giving us a profit of £80,000.

Was I glad that I bought the property? Yes. Would I have bought it if I had seen it and had the locals discourage me? Perhaps no. Would I have made the eighty odd thousand pounds? NO! What would have been the reason for that? Obviously, FEAR.

My relationship with Mr. Money

Finally, I give back. I believe in the philosophy that a measure of your success is determined by the amount of people you have positively influenced. I have invested a great deal of resources into community development programs, both directly and indirectly. I use my platforms to achieve this, and also support already-established organisations who lend themselves to these same objectives.

Consequentially, I realised that the more I engage in these initiatives, the more success-creating opportunities present themselves. Regardless of that being our intended outcome, I do this because I have learnt how to relate with money. I give it away without any fear.

I remember when I first came into this country in the year 2000. I didn't have the right immigration documents to work with, so I had to do anything I could lay my hands on. I found some serious hard work as a labourer on a building site out of desperation. On the second day at the job, I was very upset that I had to do that sort of a job for money.

I went home, I was living with my sister then, and I think I actually cried. We used to have this signed timesheet that they give to us daily and that's what you submitted to the agency for you to get paid. If you don't submit the timesheets, you don't get paid.

I said to myself this is not what I want to do for money and I tore the timesheets that day. My sister was mad at me. She felt I was really stupid because I had already done the hard work. She said, "Yes, you can decide not to go there again, but at least get paid for the job you have already done."

I actually tore up the pay-slip. Thinking back now, I believe it was me trying to prove that until I could demonstrate that I had no fear of money, money would not freely come to me. So now I am not afraid to distribute it, to reinvest, to give back, because for some strange reason Mr. Money knows who's not afraid of him and he somehow finds his way to those people.

THE POWER OF SUPERIOR SERVICE

The irreplaceable Maya Angelou said, *"People will forget what you said, they will forget what you did, but they will never forget how you made them feel."*

Now, this is one of the greatest secrets to entrepreneurial success, making people feel great and killing them with service. As your enterprise grows and includes many staff and employees, it is critical you teach them this principle from the very start of their induction process.Great service is a culture that stems from the very top. It will rub off on the entire organisation if you will make it important and a habit.

As at the time of writing this chapter in mid-April 2017, I had just returned from my second business trip to the beautiful Golf State of Kuwait. I have been working for the past few months with two high-profile members of the royal family as their life coach. It is one of the most exciting and amazing experiences ever, because royalty is a far cry from government and business entities, which is my usual experience.

However, once you receive and enjoy royal treatment, you do not want to revert to 'normal' anymore. They really pull out the stops. Every need and attention is catered for from high-level priority meet and greet at the airport, to every conceivable comfort you can imagine, plus an assigned personal shopper who took me out and negotiated the prices of goods, plus paid for the items I bought on behalf of the palace. I was not allowed to dip my hands into my pocket.

Now, since I operate a speaking, coaching and training business, I am not unaccustomed to high-profile clients and luxuries. I have been privileged to host presidents, prime ministers, captains of industry, and extremely revered spiritual leaders in my career. However it just isn't the same when you engage with true royalty.

The reason I am telling you this story is because a great lady, whom I had the pleasure to serve as a client, introduced me to the royal family. This lady attended one of the top finishing schools in Switzerland with one of the Kuwaiti princesses thirty years prior. When the Princess came to London and was looking for somebody to solve some problems, the lady informed her she knew just the man. One of my videos was quickly sent to the Princess. She checked it out and asked to meet with me promptly.

Within 72 hours, we had met face-to-face. After a brief chat, she engaged my services, and she also said,

"Oh, by the way, I think my mum would like to meet you, too. I met with her mum, one of the most significant figures and sheroes (female version of heroes) in the entire Golf region, and she also retained my services. They are now like family to me. They are an extremely humble, kind, and generous family with their staggering wealth.

I cannot stress enough the importance of serving your clients or customers with everything you have. Let us remember that there are three powerful things driving this current knowledge and information age, and these are:

1. Quality information

2. Technology

3. Competition

The world has never been as competitive as it is right now. It is a big and costly mistake to take your customers for granted when there are plenty of happy, enthusiastic, competitive people who will happily look after your customers with speed, better pricing, and a smile.

I have never been able to understand why many entrepreneurs and businesses do not go all out to serve their clients? Yes, I know there are some very difficult clients, but for every difficult client, there are usually 20 great ones.

THE IMPORTANCE OF YOUR CUSTOMERS

I remember running a series of 'customer service excellence' trainings for the immigration and customer facing staff of the Nigeria High Commission in London over a period of five years. This is one of the top two Missions in the world in terms of size, influence, and impact. On one of the training sessions with the High Commissioner himself in attendance, I proceeded to give this hypothetical situation as an example and requested for their feedback.

I asked them to imagine for a moment that they, the staff, came to work as usual, opened the doors to the public, and were ready to serve them. However, right through the entire day the phones did not ring, and nobody showed up for anything. Nobody came for visas, nobody came to report a lost passport, or sought help with an emergency travel certificate. Nobody came to renew an expired passport, nobody came with their children or spouse to change names or have names added to their passports, nobody came to enquire from the trade and industry section about the rules and guidelines to operate business in Nigeria for foreign entities looking to expand operations to that dynamic market.

There were no enquiries from Her Majesty's Foreign Office, no phone calls, let alone physical visitors; the entire Mission was very quiet. Now the same situation occurred again the next day, and all through the week, and one month later the same problem. No one ringing, no one enquiring or purchasing any services. The staff kept coming in to work as normal, but had nothing to do, and just hung around waiting for something to happen.

Now truthfully at this point, what is beginning to go through your mind as a leader? What is going through your staff's mind? Firstly, I believe your staff members will begin to speak among themselves and begin to panic as their jobs may be at risk and they will begin to feel vulnerable. Just think about it for a moment.

Your staff members have rents or mortgages to pay every month. They probably have families to feed and clothe, transportation and travel costs, credit card bills, electricity, and gas to pay for monthly. They have council tax bills every month, and for some, money to send to elderly relatives, medical bills, children's shoes, school uniforms, school fees, and other incidentals. Now all these expenses and costs are all dependent on the money they receive from their employment.

The very people who are responsible for providing the opportunity for their employment are the customers. Customers are the life blood of the business. Yet they are treated without proper consideration, care, and respect, when their very livelihood depends on the patronage of these same customers!

Secondly, you the leader, proprietor, or principal business owner will probable begin to wonder how long this paucity of patronage will continue. Now, imagine one month later, the phones finally began to ring, and people began to show up for one request or the other. How would you treat them now? I bet they would probably receive the best service they have ever experienced!

I bet so much love, appreciation, and consideration will be poured out on them. This is how you need to treat them all the time! The businesses enjoying superior patronage and growth have got this figured out, and you need to make this a most vital part of your business.

Your business is nothing without clients or customers. Everything revolves around the customer. Customers truly are kings and queens, whether you are a hotel, restaurant, store, plastic surgeon, a cable network provider, radio station, management consultant, accountant, hospital, bank, trainer and coach, church, mosque, fashion designer, software developer, shoe manufacturer, internet marketer, nutritional product manufacturer, weight management companies and the list is endless. Without customers, your enterprise is nothing!

So if the above is true, then one wonders why there are so many terrible businesses taking very poor care of their customers? It is your responsibility, just as Richard Branson and Oprah and every other highly successful entrepreneur does, to train your employees to understand that repeat business is the life blood of any enterprise. Your goal is to get the customer coming back for more. Do not just focus on one time sales.

HOW I DEVELOPED A SOLID BRAND AS THE GO TO GUY FOR INTERNATIONAL HIGH PROFILE EVENTS

I have succeeded in developing a strong brand as a speaker and international events compere/ facilitator by simply delivering far more than what I am paid. Today, I probably command one of the highest fees in my profession for these events because I have proven my value over the past 10 years in this space.

I can honestly tell you now that I have never knowingly lost a client. The only time a client chooses not to use my services, is either because they have no budget for it, or they cannot afford it, and they usually inform me. Sometimes, depending on the event, I have proceeded to offer my services gratis. And when I offer my services for free, I usually deliver it as if I was being paid my full fees.

There are so many people who believe they owe me up until this day, because they were not in a financial position to pay me. The good will I have generated and the positive brand endorsement I have received is far more than the money.

The profit of your business from the start to the end will be driven by the customer. Ensure you put customer service at the heart of everything you do. A positive recommendation from a satisfied and happy client will steer dozens more your way.

This is one of the most credible forms of publicity for your business, and every time a customer recommends your business, they are also putting their own credibility on the line and you don't want to embarrass them with poor service delivery.

HOW TO DEVELOP GREAT CUSTOMER SERVICE 10 QUICK TIPS

1. Train your employees on superior customer service philosophy. Make it a priority to indoctrinate all your employees on a customer first philosophy. Ensure they understand the customers are the life blood of the business. Teach the employees that their very existence depends on the patronage of both new and returning customers.

2. Don't make a promise that you cannot keep. If you promise your customer something, then go all out to fulfil it, even if it costs you.

3. If you make a mistake, apologise and promptly make amends. Customers are sensible human beings; they know mistakes can be made. The most important is the ability to resolve it with an apology or great gesture. This will build great trust between you and the customer.

4. Never ignore the presence of a customer. If you have a business that attracts walk- in customers, whatever you or your staff are doing, stop immediately and acknowledge the presence of the customer, always with a welcoming smile.

Never ignore their presence or scowl and blurt, "Yes? Can I help you?" Instead, look them in the eye with a warm smile and ask, "How can I help?"

5. Deal with their complaints promptly. Even though no one likes dealing with complaints, you have to do this. It is critical to your short, immediate, and long-term success. Always endeavour to deal with the customer complaint the first time.

Desist from passing them round and round to different people. Customers dislike intensely having to call over and over again to resolve same problem. It is one of their biggest frustrations, and it stops many from coming back to you if they can help it.

6. Know what your customers want. Listen to the complaints, requests, or suggestions from customers and aim to satisfy them if doable. Find out what is important to your customers and do more of it. Make customer feedback mechanisms available.

7. Know the ins and outs of your products or service, or at least have sufficient knowledge of them.

Customers cannot stand employees who do not know their products and cannot give good and helpful advice when required by customers.

8.   Introduce yourself intentionally. Put a personal touch by introducing yourself to the customer. Let them put a name and face to the business and they will get used to calling you on a first name basis.

Nothing reassures customers as much as the owner of the business coming out to shake their hands and offer his or her personal service. No matter how big your business gets, make a choice to do this periodically.

9.   Make it easy to locate customer support. Customers find it extremely infuriating, having conducted business with your company, when then cannot find support when they have a problem. Provide a contact telephone number and an email contact address with a promise of how long it takes to respond to their enquiry.

10.   Find a way of creating unique and VIP services for your best customers. Let them know they are your best customers and are very important to your business. This could be in the form of special promotions, gifts, or first-to-know incentives and the like.

Chapter Fourteen:

The Power Of A Mentor For Your Business Success

"Where there is no counsel plans fail, but in a multitude of wise counsellors, there is safety."
- *Proverbs 15:22*

I had my first business mentor in 1996 at a company convention in Memphis, Tennessee. I had just been appointed into the prestigious President's Advisory Council (PAC10) with NSA/Juice Plus. The convention had thousands of people, and there were company superstars all over the huge auditorium. Lots of millionaires from all over the world were there.

The event had key and selected speakers going on stage to speak and share their wisdom with the crowd. All of a sudden this gentleman, Kerry Daigle, went up to speak. Instantly, I was drawn to him. We were both at the same rank of National Marketing Director, the top position in the company; however, he had a much larger and more mature business, while I was newly promoted.

I had some of my key leaders from the UK with me, and when I spotted Kerry later, I went up to introduce myself with my team. When he saw my pin (rank) he said to me that I was a very humble guy to be asking for mentorship even though I was already at the top.

He then turned to my team and told them to listen to me and to follow my example. Kerry was a millionaire from the business. He was and is also a big time successful boxing promoter.

Kerry took a liking to me and I requested officially for him to be my business mentor, which he graciously accepted. He is an American Cajun, an ethnic group which are descendants of Acadian exiles (French-speakers from Acadia Eastern Canada).

He has a larger-than-life presence with a happy, booming laughter. He soon introduced me immediately to everyone, saying "this is my friend, Charles

Khiran. He is a champion from England, Great Britain."

Kerry taught me succinct and specialised marketing skills. He opened my mind, mainly to his unique way of making people feel really important. I observed the subtle little things he did and the effects of those things on people, I watched how he communicated with everybody and learned rare skills instantly, purely from observation. I picked up many things from him, plus I was able to call him every month for a few years, and he would always give me tips on one thing or the other.

I actually felt very rich just having Kerry in my corner. I would talk to everyone back in Europe about him, and many also had a lot of admiration for him. I still call him my mentor until this day, and we stay in touch mainly via Facebook now.

Wise mentors have been there, done it, and have seen it all. Yet it is really surprising that many entrepreneurs start their businesses without seeking a mentor. Somebody once said that spending 30 minutes across the table with a wise mentor is worth more than reading several books...wow! What a profound statement? However, that is the true power of a great mentor.

The idea of mentorship is to seek out individuals who are strong, experienced, and successful in the particular area you are lacking. There is a substantial difference between learning theories from many people and being personally mentored.

If you are fortunate enough to have a great mentor, you will discover it is a far more valuable experience than any formal education....honestly!

MY MENTORS

I am proud to say I have several spiritual and success mentors, some of them from a distance. At the front of this book I acknowledge many of them. However, I have also had about 3 financial mentors in my life to date. None of them is greater than my current one, who became my mentor in 2014. This gentleman is a billionaire with many substantial businesses in over 53 countries.

I have learnt much more about wealth and business in the past 3 years of our close friendship than reading many books. By simply spending quality time with this individual, observing, and listening as he engages with the lowly through to the high and mighty in society. From the way he negotiates business deals, to the way he uses his generosity to transform lives and wow people.

Most of all for somebody worth so much money, I have learnt through pure observation the power of his disarming humility and how he puts money in the right perspectives. More than anything else my vision, which I thought was already quite big, has been stretched to unbelievable levels as I observe this gentleman operate like nothing is truly impossible.

I have, for example, sat in board meetings with him and observed his negotiating power. I have also watched as he tackles substantial business deals that would normally defy human logic. I have seen the energy he exerts, sometimes until the wee hours of the morning, closing deals with no loss of enthusiasm. I cannot quantify easily the benefits from our various conversations across the dinner table or in the car on our various travels. It has been completely life changing even at this stage in my life!

WHAT IS A MENTOR?

Let us begin first with a definition of a mentor. The Mariam-Webster dictionary defines a 'mentor' as a trusted counsellor or guide. A mentor is somebody who is very experienced and successful in the area you want to develop. This can be a business or career mentor, which is our topic in this chapter; however, you can have mentors in various aspects of your life; you could have a spiritual mentor, financial mentor, success mentor, marriage mentor, fitness mentor, health & wellness mentor, and so on. However, the type of mentorship I am discussing in this chapter is not a professional or fee-paying mentorship, which is available in the market.

Career mentors are extremely popular in the corporate world and in the public sector. The dynamics in career mentoring is similar to business mentoring. The difference with career mentoring is that the process happens within a corporate or job environment with a view of furthering the upward trajectory of the mentee in the organisation. This, of course, is a win-win for both the organisation and the mentee. The organisation benefits from the possibilities of having talented and well-groomed individuals in the pipeline to aid in succession planning.

The mentee also benefits by potentially having his or her career fast- tracked because of the knowledge and wisdom acquired from the process. Many organisations encourage senior players to make it a habit of identifying future potentials and dedicating some time to them.

The difference in business mentoring is that the mentee is a business owner or an entrepreneur seeking the guidance of successful business people. Many of the big names out there have had mentors, including the late Jim Rohn, Tony Robbins, Mark Zuckerberg, Oprah, John Maxwell, the late Myles Munroe, and so many others.

There are instances where a mentor will take it upon himself or herself to choose an individual and provide mentorship. However, what is more common especially in business, is the person who is in need of help, goes out and actively seek a mentor.

I must add, at this stage, that not all mentors say yes. These are very busy individuals, especially the highly successful ones, and they just might not be motivated to say yes. My advice to you is that once you have identified a potential mentor, go to them and ask politely if they would consider being your mentor.

Here are some things I suggest you say to them:

• "You are one of the most admired people I know. I believe I can truly succeed if I have somebody like you to point me in the right direction. Would you consider mentoring me very occasionally, even from a distance, as I know you are a very busy man/lady?"

• "I have a head full of dreams and I have made measurable progress so far, but I know if I had the benefit of your wisdom and guidance, I could definitely reach for the stars"

• "I know I am capable of becoming truly successful; however, there are a few areas where I really struggle. If I could speak to you occasionally when I get stuck, it would mean the world to me"

If they say yes to the occasional phone calls or contact, it may lead to full blown-out mentoring sessions if you handle it well. Remember, you are not paying any fees for their time, so it is purely based on good will.

Offer to pay for lunch or dinner or whatever works to give you the benefit of their time. Remember, do not accept NO easily! If they say NO to you, thank them and try again. Keep trying until they change their minds or you discover you are being a nuisance.

Only then should you stop asking. Sometimes, just by persisting, you may impress the potential mentor of your seriousness to be mentored by them.

As the Webster's dictionary defines above, mentors are trusted counsellors, which mean they play a pivotal role in a mentee's life and success.

WHAT CAN A MENTOR DO FOR YOU?

One of the first tasks of your mentor is to clarify what type of developmental needs you have. Then, set some goals and achievable objectives in other to measure the effectiveness of the process.

Think for a moment what you can achieve with a good teacher or coach. If you are able to achieve or increase your success, say by 70%, with a superb teacher or coach, a mentor can take you upwards of 1000% and above! A real mentor who is worth his or her salt can deliver electrifying and life-changing value to you from their treasure trove of experience, knowledge, and wisdom.

Using the arena of business as an example, a business mentor is somebody who has been very successful in business. Chances are they know how to guide you through the minefields of business. They know how to deliver solid advice to you and ask you the hard questions to get your mental juices flowing in the right direction regarding a myriad of business related issues.

A business mentor is usually older, but not all the time. There are many successful business people who are younger, too. What a mentee is after is the experience and the wealth of knowledge the mentor brings to the table. I have mentored many people in various areas over the decades.

I chose carefully now in whom I invest my time and energy. My most frequent requests are from people who want to learn the art of public speaking, entrepreneurship, or leadership and life success related issues. Later in this chapter, I shall list out what a mentor looks for in a mentee.

The role of the mentor is simply to guide and provide advice to the mentee. The mentee has the privilege of observing and asking questions to the mentor while the mentor provides guidance through assessing, appraising, challenging, and supporting the mentee.

A mentor can enable you to make quantum leaps in your business by stopping you from making errors and costly mistakes based on their own experiences. Also, they can provide you with the confidence to shoot for the stars, and will be there to pick you up should you come crashing to the floor.

A mentor is somebody who is safe, and you can share your deep thoughts and visions with, as they are not threatened by your dreams and can be trusted.

THE MENTOR AND MENTEE RELATIONSHIP

If you are fortunate to secure a great mentor, then realise they are very busy people. From my experience, mentors don't like wasting their time, and will usually appraise you carefully to see if you are somebody they want to invest time and energy into.

They are usually drawn to mentees they believe have potential. If they don't think so, they will politely fob you off. Even when they believe you have potential, they still need to be persuaded you are worth their time.

THE ROLE AND RESPONSIBILITIES OF THE MENTEE

1.   The mentee must show gratitude, courtesy, and respect to the mentor at all times, and be prepared to work and commit to raising your game.

2.   Your responsibility as a mentee is to extract as much knowledge as you can from your mentor. You must desire to absorb as much knowledge and wisdom from them as possible.

3.   Your mentor may be for a season in your life, or it may be life-long depending on your relationship. So it is incumbent on you, the mentee, to pick up as much as possible in the fastest possible time to set you up for maximum success.

4.   Make a habit of writing down key nuggets from your sessions and interactions. Also, remember most of the important things are caught and not taught. Pay close attention to their EQ (Emotional Intelligence), how they handle people around them, how they deal with disappointments, their outlook on life, how they control and discipline emotions, etc. A lot of your success will be down to how you manage your emotions and deal with disappointments, so pay particular attention to this.

5.   Don't do too much talking. Defer to your mentor, who has the knowledge, wisdom, and information you are seeking. Chances are he is not there for you to show off how much you know. Instead, speak less and listen much.

6.   Ask intelligent questions. The quality of your questions will give your mentor an idea of the size of your mind. Direct most of your questions to the areas where you require the most help.

7.   When your mentor gives you any task, be sure you act on it quickly. This will give your mentor confidence that you are a good student. Remember, some mentors will test you to see if you followed through on the last instruction they gave you.

8.   Please remember the mentor's role is not to do the work for you. However, if they choose to, for example, open up their networks to you, or introduce you to any specific person, that is a bonus and not part of the deal.

9.   Also remember the mentor is not there to give you money or bail you out of your financial situation. However, if they choose to want to invest in your busi-

ness or bail you out, that is a blessing, but not part of the mentoring process.

10. Always volunteer to pay for the drinks if you are meeting outside of the office or home, unless they insist on paying.

Chapter Fifteen:

Fostering A Global Dominating Mind-Set

"The empires of the future will be empires of the mind"

- Sir Winston Churchill

Fr. Pierre Teilhard de Chardin, a French Jesuit priest who trained as a palaeontologist and philosopher, said, "It is our duty as men and women to proceed as though limits to our abilities do not exist. We are collaborators in creation."

For most intents and purposes, the spirit and creativity of the human being is limitless if properly utilised and channelled. You and I were meant to use our entrepreneurial skills and talents to serve the world. You were meant to answer or satisfy a problem in the world with your entrepreneurial gifts, and that is the bigger picture. It is bigger than just the desire to make a profit or become famous.

Yes, it is true that power and staggering wealth can be achieved through the vehicle of business. However, the most important reason for setting up in business is to add value to the world by serving humanity and transforming lives with your unique gifts and ideas. A great example of serving humanity with your gifts and ideas is Mark Zuckerberg.

Mark invented Facebook initially with three of his Harvard classmates. Originally it was just an idea for connecting friends at Harvard and surrounding colleges. None of them knew how hugely successful it was going to become.

The incredible power of the Facebook platform cannot be over emphasized. It has connected billions of long lost friends and acquaintances around the world. It has given power back to the people to broadcast themselves like never before free of charge. It has created millions of indirect jobs around the world through the marketing, managing, and utilisation of his platform.

It is estimated that 1 out of 7 people around the world use Facebook. It has created a massive gold mine for advertisers who cannot believe their luck, as it enables them to properly build profiles and target people and their friends with lightening results for their clients.

Facebook has also been a great platform for unheard voices to be heard as they broadcast themselves, from complaining about bad service of a brand to actually creating mass movements of protests against governments and political parties. As a matter of fact, many political parties and governments now target people through Facebook to spread their messages.

President Obama famously had huge and unrivalled success when his campaign team mobilised young people and created an unstoppable movement through Facebook which resulted in an unprecedented victory for Obama in his first presidency. Facebook has made it possible for entrepreneurs like me to build a free online profile and reach nations far and wide with my messages of hope, superior human productivity, and empowerment.

The same dynamic is true for other famous social media platforms like Twitter, Instagram, and YouTube. The medium of YouTube is successfully challenging traditional television stations by allowing billions of people to effectively create their own television channels and broadcast their own messages to the world population free of charge.

YouTube has shrunk the world by making it smaller. Just by a single click, we can travel anywhere around the world, and educate ourselves about literally anything.

YouTube is also making manufacturer's manuals obsolete or unnecessary as better information and tutorials are provided for almost anything, with humans patiently lecturing on how to succeed on any given issue. Whether it is baking cakes or bread, braiding or treating your hair, homemade recipes for optimum health, how to lose weight and manage your nutrition, how to fix your camera, how other cultures live, how to fix a broken part of a car or motorcycle to catching snakes or crabs.

Literally anything you can think of there is a YouTube video addressing it comprehensibly. Now I know I have focused a lot on technology, but the same can be said for almost anything from launching a budget airline, to reducing the exorbitant costs of air travel, to insurance to protect us from loss, to making it easier for humans to communicate in far distant lands through the power of mobile phones, to a myriad of time saving or life giving ideas around the world.

Entrepreneurs are making these happen and changing the face of the world by bringing untold quality, sophistication, and dignity to human lives. Now, because these intrepid entrepreneurs gamble everything they have on bringing the world their ideas and concepts, when they succeed, the world in turn rewards them staggeringly whether with unthinkable wealth, power, and influence. However, they first had to bring their ideas to the table and hold their breath, with some losing everything in the process, before success was realised.

With every business comes a customer or client population that requires service and to have their needs met. Some of these may be local, restricted to a geographical location, while others may be regional, and some global. What is critical for you to note however is, even if your business is local or regional, you must continually think global. More than anything technology has made it possible to compete globally now with more ease and less red tape.

As the great American essayist, poet, and philosopher Henry David Thoreau said "If one advances confidently in the direction of their dreams, and endeavour to live the life that they have imagined, they shall meet with a success unexpected in common hours"

Here are some people doing just that with a global dominating mind-set and shooting for the stars.

OLIVIA LUM: CHAIRMAN & GROUP CEO HY-FLUX (A TRUE RAGS TO RICHES STORY)

This is the powerful story of a lady who went literally from rags to super riches, from an orphan to a super multimillionaire entrepreneur. Olivia was born in Malaysia and was abandoned by birth at the hospital. She was adopted by a woman she called grandmother, but sadly the grandmother was a gambler, and blew all her money when Olivia was an infant.

They had to move out of their comfortable house into an attap hut with bare earth and no running water or electricity. She had to travel to a well every day to fetch water, most of which was spilt even before she got home. She hated this chore very much.

Her memorable childhood was characterised by

mind numbing poverty and hardship. It would seem those difficulties prepared her for the challenges ahead and the uncommon determination which has seen her succeed against the odds to staggering heights.

At the age of nine, her grandmother could not sustain her anymore as she became too old to work. Olivia became the sole bread winner and would sell anything from fruits, sandwiches, and ice cream to earn money. Olivia was very gifted academically and was advised by her school master to try and get herself to Singapore where she could have greater opportunities for advancement.

At age 15, she hustled her way to Singapore to continue her education. When she arrived, she was rejected by several schools, but eventually succeeded in gaining admission with one. To pay her tuition, she worked at different jobs like waitressing and private tutoring to earn money for her fees.

She eventually gained admission to the prestigious National University of Singapore, and yet again supported herself by selling souvenirs, cosmetics, and insurance. Some of the extra money she earned was invested in partnership canteen ventures at construction sites.

She did well with the food business and, by the end of her time at university, Olivia was one of the few students who owned a car. She graduated with an honours degree in Chemistry in 1986.

Her first proper job was with Glaxo pharmaceuticals, as she could not launch her entrepreneurial dreams due to the recession at that time. She got a more stable employment as a laboratory chemist with the giant company working in a section engaged in the disposal of waste water in the drug making process. Olivia could not believe the vast amounts of money spent on the in-house water treatment. She saw that it was a great business to be in.

In the eighties, the public awareness in Asian countries about water pollution was growing. She also discovered, during her time at Glaxo, the huge potential in water treatment and recycling in water deprived Singapore.

Then, in 1989 at the age of 29, she left her well-paid job and launched out on her own, selling her condo and her car to raise money. She also attracted some investment money from some people and she was able to raise the seed capital of $20,000 to found Hyflux, initially called Hydrochem, with only one clerk and a technician.

Initially Hydrochem traded in water filters and softners, but she knew in order for her to grow, she had to go into manufacturing armed with the highest technological capabilities. Olivia visited her lecturers at her old University seeking solutions, and the University agreed to help her develop the technology.

She visited Israel and met a professor who introduced her to water membrane technology. She returned to Singapore with the new membrane technology in 1993 and introduced it to the market. Hyflux was able to secure some orders from various quarters, but her first big break came when she secured a large order from Siemens Matsushita Components. Her business and her company's reputation took off from there. In 2001 Hyflux became the first water treatment company in Singapore to be listed on the SGX SESDAQ.

A new benchmark was also set in 2011 when Hyflux was awarded the contract to build Singapore's second and largest seawater desalination project. In 2015, Hyflux partnered with Mitsubishi Heavy Industries to design and build Singapore's sixth waste-to-energy plant.

Hyflux has been successfully conducting huge businesses from China, India, and Saudi Arabia. Recently, in March 2016, Hyflux was awarded a US$500-million project, commissioned by the General Authority for the Suez Canal Economic Zone, to construct the Ain Sokhna Integrated Water and Power plant in Egypt.

Hyflux employs over 2500 employees and over $700 million USD in turnover last year (2016)

Olivia was ranked number 27 out of the top 40 richest people in Singapore with a net worth of $460 million according to Forbes. She is the only woman who made the list.

Here is a selection of her achievements and awards:

- 2003: Singapore's Ernst & Young Entrepreneur of the Year award

- Winner the Nikkei Asia Prize for Regional Growth 2006

- 2004: Businesswoman of the Year by the Singapore Business Awards

- 2010: Ernst & Young Singapore Entrepreneur of the Year award

- Ernst & Young World Entrepreneur Of The Year 2011

- Financial Times Arcelor Mittal Boldness in Business Award 2011 for Entrepreneurship

STRIVE MASIYIWA, FOUNDER & CHAIRMAN OF ECONET WIRELESS

One such man with a global mind-set, boldly dominating his space, is the exceptional leader, Strive Masiyiwa. Zimbabwe's richest man, with a fortune estimated at $600 million by some and others estimate his wealth as high as $1.4 billion US, he is the founder, chairman, and CEO of Econet Wireless, a global telecoms group headquartered in South Africa.

It is estimated that a large portion of his fortune comes from his stake in Econet. His telecoms company is Zimbabwe's largest telecoms provider with approximately 9 million users. It has operations in 18 countries, and investments in telecoms in New Zealand and the USA.

Strive first rose to international prominence when he successfully challenged the Zimbabwean government in a gruelling 5-year legal battle to break the government's monopoly in the market. The success of the legal challenge paved the way for Strive to launch his own telecom company. Strive is one of Africa's most respected business leaders and one of the key leaders at the forefront of advancing key sectors like financial services, insurance, renewable energy, hotels, and safari lodges.

This impressive gentleman has a huge following of many young professionals who see him as a key role model, both for his sharp intellect and his passion for philanthropy, which has endeared many to him. He is an ardent campaigner against corruption in Africa and the championing of the rule of law.

Strive and his wife, Tsitsi, runs a foundation, The Higher Life, which provides scholarships to over 25,000 destitute orphans in Zimbabwe. He is also a tireless educator and promoter of the awareness and impact of AIDS. Strive is a trustee of the Rockefeller Foundation and a board member of the Alliance for a Green Revolution in Africa.

SIZA MZIMELA, FOUNDER & CEO OF FLY BLUE CRANE

Siza's full names are Sizakele Petunia Mzimela. She made history by becoming the first Black woman to own an airline when she launched Fly Blue Crane airline in South Africa. Siza worked in the aviation industry for years, beginning her career with SAA in 1997 as a market analyst, and rose to the very top, making history in South Africa.

Siza recorded several firsts, as she was also the first female CEO of South African Airways in its history, serving from 2010 – 2012. This powerful lady also became the first female to be appointed to the board of the International Air Transport Association (AITA) board of directors in 67 years.

Under Siza's inspirational leadership, in her first year in charge SAA, direct flights to New York and Beijing were introduced for the first time. SAA also expanded its regional networks by an additional eight regions in one year.

Siza launched her airline, Fly Blue Crane, in September 2015 in partnership with Tambo International Airport in Johannesburg. Siza, as can be expected, has been an incredible role model for many people, especially Black women who sees limitless possibilities with hard work and determination, regardless of colour or prejudice. Siza also sits on the Oprah Winfrey Leadership Academy for Girls.

BE PREPARED FOR SUDDEN GROWTH

The late and irreplaceable motivational speaker, Zig Ziglar, once told a story about a biscuit that got cooked in the squat. He said that after his mum put the biscuit dough on a tray and placed them in the oven, the biscuit was trying to rise. Unfortunately, before it could properly rise it got cooked in the squat and came out a bit wonky. I am sure you can see the picture in your mind of what happened to that unfortunate biscuit.

The same lesson we must learn from poor and improper preparation. A particular American company many years ago was the rage in helping women to reshape their bodies by fitting into garments, dropping up to 3 dress sizes. This great concept and product helped to reshape, lift, and smooth out troubled areas in the woman's body without surgery. It was an instant hit.

Based on the success in the US, they began expanding internationally without making adequate preparation. The business exploded here in the UK. Africa, Jamaica, and other places followed. They could not keep up with the demand.

Customers were having to wait for months to receive products and, after an incredible start, disappointments followed. People could not get their products on time. The company became overwhelmed, distributors were owed a lot of money, and the brand and reputation of the company suffered considerably.

Very soon, cheap Chinese imitations of their product flooded the market. A golden opportunity was missed by the company for what should undoubtedly have become a multi-billion dollar business. Instead, its reputation suffered and distributors left in the thousands.

What was the lesson they should have learnt? They should have prepared for expansion. Instead, they were caught in the squat.

Your preparation before sudden expansion is critical. In the process of your usual business activities, keep an eye out for potential opportunities that can expand or explode your business. Let me explain a particular situation that happened to me about 10 years ago. I had been actively networking and creating very strong and influential contacts and I had been spending a lot of time in prayer seeking divine assistance.

However, I had no idea that my prayers and active networking was about to yield immediate fruits. All of a sudden I received a phone call from an African client who wanted to send 50 senior members from a financial institution to London for a high level financial instruments training within 10 days, plus an excursion to some key places of interests while in London.

Unfortunately some of our African clients don't

give you much time to prepare. You have to be on the ball and ready, as they could call anytime and say we are coming. Then, it will be up to you to do the running around and accommodate their request if you want the business.

It was a big deal financially speaking, approximately £170,000 in value. However, there was no way I could respond in time plus deliver the quality required. I was very tempted to deliver the project, but because of the seniority of the delegates I knew they would spot poor quality and inadequate preparation.

Sadly, I passed it on to a more established organisation who had the capacity and staff to handle such a big deal. I got a referral fee plus a little share of the profit. I remember it to this day, but it was a very valuable lesson to learn.

So what I did immediately after that event was to put in place strategic partners and affiliates that I could call upon for some of the heavy lifting should the need arise. I have since, of course, grown to the point where I can handle much bigger opportunities in my organisation.

Now I know some of you would probably be thinking, "If I were in your shoes, I would have risked it and done the business yourself."

Yes, I could have done that, but I could also have ruined my brand and reputation by creating confusion and disappointing this high level client. My reputation probably would not have recovered for a long time.

So here is the lesson, as you test out your ideas in

the market, some may be breakthrough ideas. Without warning, people can begin responding to your business. Instead of the usual small numbers of clients, it explodes to 3 or 4 times the normal, and you begin to panic over how to accommodate the new increase as you do not have the capacity.

One thing everybody learns quickly is that customers can be very unforgiving when they are let down. Take time to plan adequately for any potential sudden increase or at least have a backup plan in place for any positive eventualities.

The great Winston Churchill said *"There comes a special moment in a person's life, when they are figuratively tapped on the shoulders and offered the opportunity to do something really special, unique to them and fitted to their talents. What a tragedy it would be if that moment comes and finds them unprepared or unqualified for that which could have been their finest hour"*

To your great success!

About the Author

Connect with Charles Online
LinkedIn: http://bit.ly/2wYRMAU
Facebook: http://bit.ly/2wbKUAt
YouTube: http://bit.ly/2fkOEFf

Charles Ajayi-Khiran is the Founder & Principal consultant of 3cjglobal and Charles Khiran International, a corporate training, Executive Coaching, and Professional Speaking organisation.

Charles has been a successful entrepreneur for over 2 decades, as somebody who has failed several times in business, including experiencing bankruptcy; he understands experientially what it takes to succeed. Charles has personally consulted and coached over 400 senior executives and CEO's on career and business success.

He has developed sales professionals and entrepreneurs of approximately 40,000 in his business over the past 27 years. He is advisor to governments, royalty, captains of Industry, Civic and church leaders. He is a highly successful international speaker of conviction, focusing on leadership, entrepreneurship, inspiration and empowerment.

Charles is married and blessed with 2 children and they make their home in London, UK